Much Love
Cathilu + Melissa
♡

Freedom Rising From Within

The Ultimate Guide to Freedom & Transformation From the Inside-Out

Cathrine Marshall & Melissa Lyons

There is no greater gift we can offer ourselves, future generations, and the planet than the dedication toward our own personal transformation.

It is through our loving and steady commitment to this mission that we will create our own legacy and a world worthy of leaving behind.

We dedicate this book to you, the Awakened Seeking Soul.

May your path of remembering be inspiring.

May your heart ablaze with passion.

May you go forth in your brilliance.

May your mind be illumined.

Cathrine and Melissa 2022

Please note: At times our journey will bring up challenging emotions and memories. May you know you are always loved and supported, even in the darkest and loneliest of times.

Please seek additional or professional support if needed.

Publisher's Notes

This publication is designed to support personal spiritual development and growth with respect to the subject matter presented. Neither the publisher nor the authors intend this book for the rendering of medical, psychological or other professional services, prescriptions or advice. If there is a need for expert services beyond the scope of this book, please seek out the services of a medical professional. This book is offered for information purposes only.

Freedom Rising Within – The Ultimate Guide to Freedom & Transformation From the Inside-Out
Published by Choose to Choose Inc., Kingsville ON Canada

Copyright 2022 by Cathrine Marshall and Melissa Lyons

Illustrations by Kerri McCabe. Reproduced with her permission.

Printed in China, 1st Edition

Traditional Book ISBN: 978-1-7773843-0-2
E-Book ISBN: 978-1-7773843-2-6
Audiobook ISBN: 978-1-7773843-1-9

SEL042000	SELF-HELP / Emotions
SEL021000	SELF-HELP / Motivational & Inspirational
OCC019000	BODY, MIND & SPIRIT / Inspiration & Personal Growth

TABLE OF CONTENTS

The power of love is here now
The power of now is here now
The power of you and me is here to create magic on earth

Let the water wash away your tears
Let the fire burn away your fears
Let the wind blow into your life such faith and trust
Let the earth hold you, take care of you, nurture you

The power of love is here now
The power of now is here now
The power of you and me is here to create magic on earth

Song: The Power is Here Now
By: Alexia Chellun
Album: Just Before I Sleep

Introducton

We are on a path of **Conscious Return**. To our wisdom, compassion, sovereignty, and regality. The time of the Power of Love is upon us. As such, we are in process of a mass, evolutionary collective awakening. Navigating through this paradigm shift, many questions arise. At our core, we are contemplating how we can experience deeper meaning, purpose, connectivity, love, peace, and freedom.

We are being roused to examine our impact on the environment, the legacy we are leaving our future generations, and how we can alleviate the pervasive injustice and suffering that permeates so much of this world.

We may find ourselves reaching for the most important answers to the overriding questions: *Is it even possible to change ourselves, humanity, or the environment? Can we really experience more love, compassion, kindness, and equality? Can we really make enough of a difference to create a New Earth?*

What if the answer is a resounding **YES**?

What if it's more than just possible? What if it's our Soul's burning desire to bring this into a state of being, and to do so we need to reclaim our freedom, our sovereignty, both individually and collectively?

The journey to transform ourselves and the world is a calling from our deepest essence, our **Soul Self**, to **Go Within**! **We are a microcosm of the macrocosm.** Our outer world reflects our inner world. Therefore, when we transform our inner world, our outer world responds accordingly and follows suit.

1

Our inward voyage unites us with our Soul and our Divine Blueprint, the roadmap to our own personal incarnational plan. This consists of our unique gifts, talents, and abilities, our desires, challenges, and unfinished lessons we intend to work on and much more!

We tune into and access our Soul plan by learning to listen to and honor our inner resonance, which contains our path of highest purpose and fulfillment. Because the Soul is infinite and aware of the grand choreography, what we are guided to from this resonance ultimately serves the highest and greatest good of all. Each plan is a piece of a puzzle to create a greater whole.

Going inward is also a discovery of any elements, beliefs, perceptions, conditioning, and imprinting that are keeping us in separation consciousness, to unearth anything that is keeping us from experiencing our true nature. This is **Divine Love**!

Sounds simple enough, doesn't it?

Fundamentally it is, however, not only have we been trained to ignore this calling but we've also been programmed to believe that it is selfish to do so. If this is true, that it is selfish, consider this: when we honor ourselves and follow our inner resonance, we serve Spirit, which always serves the highest, greatest good of all in mind. Furthermore, as we cultivate our relationship with our Soul and *journey within*, we become aware of the veils and illusions that have been keeping us in the conditioning of separatism, lack, suffering, and inequality. We remember we are LOVE and that we are compassionate, creative, free beings, with a much greater purpose than to create and experience suffering, conflict, war, starvation, despair, and pain.

We begin to remember who we are at our core. And this is where it begins to get interesting because we now begin a renewed process of aligning, cultivating, and expressing the higher vibrations of love, peace, harmony, joy, and more!

Why is this impactful? As Dr. David Hawkins's work proves, *1* person holding a **frequency of love** counterbalances *750,000* of those who are carrying lower frequencies of fear, anger, shame, or more. Transforming ourselves inspires us to consciously choose the alignment we want to be in. It is this alignment that then transforms the outer world! *As Within, So Without!*

As we honor ourselves, our processes, and our journeys with love, kindness, and respect, we can commit to honoring and supporting the same for others. We serve from a consciousness that initiates the profound and seemingly miraculous transformation. The more Soul-guided we become, the more we tap into our innate caring for the well-being of others and our planet and activate the **Inspired Right of Action**. When we become freer, we care more about the freedom of all, and an uplevelling of dignity occurs. **This is how we begin the evolutionary journey into a whole new way of being.**

Regardless of our conditions or circumstances, we understand that freedom means we always have the power to choose how we respond, and as a result, we can create a preferred and profound outcome.

Freedom Rising From Within

Remember Who You Are

Awaken To Your Potential

Understand Your Divine Blueprint

Fulfill Your Path Of Highest Purpose

Chapter 1:

Understanding Freedom

"It's not the waking; it's the rising."

Hozier

Can you imagine feeling more joy, ease, love, and peace? Can you imagine being free and living a life of freedom? Not only is this now possible in a way it's never been before, but it's also time for us to awaken to it and claim it!!! **IT'S TIME TO RISE!!!**

FREEDOM IS POWER. FREEDOM IS HEART POWER

True Power Comes From The Divine, Not The Ego. It is our inherent, Divine right that we are sovereign beings. We activate and claim this by awakening and opening our hearts. An unlocked heart becomes a channel for the infinite to flow through. Once heart power is sparked, authentic freedom can rise.

A closed heart is limited to the finite. Therefore, a subject to the ego, which can only access *false, illusionary power* and keeps us limited in freedom in so many ways.

Why Is This? We have been conditioned, programmed, and trained to believe and think we are limited, undeserving, and subservient. We have been in fear, separation, and asleep, and we have forgotten that our true nature is, in fact, *Divine*.

We are now in the process of shifting paradigms. As a result, we are

5

awakening to our inner Divine presence, **Our Soul Self**. Because of this, we are now invited to start accepting our birthright of freedom, which may well be our highest purpose at this current time.

WE ARE TRANSFORMING

Just like a baby/toddler/child goes through developmental stages of growth, humanity as a species is also going through this evolutionary process. Until now, the species as a collective has been operating at an adolescent level and is now evolving and leaping into the next phase of development. To better understand this, let's explore the concept of Soul and ego.

Earth School. From a spiritual perspective, we are a Soul incarnated in a body, having a human experience. This *temporary form* (body) is the vehicle thru which we navigate this experiential *school*.

The Soul takes great care in developing the body and personality for the upcoming incarnation. There is meticulous care to what is being chosen as the blueprint for learning, growing, and healing.

Think of incarnating on Earth as a particular school that we are attending for a period. The Soul learns through and experiences this school with the union of the body and personality.

The personality contains the mind and ego. There is negative ego and positive ego. Previously the ego led the personality because the purpose of the ego was to keep us alive and safe. As a collective, we were operating from the consciousness of *survive*; therefore, we needed the ego forefront.

Now, however, we are evolving into **heart consciousness**! We still need the ego while we are here incarnated; however, we are now learning to become a more **Soul-infused personality**. The ego is still necessary to some degree; otherwise, we wouldn't care about

6

evolving, serving others, or contributing. We are now learning to activate more of the positive aspect of ego, *to attend to the heart and Soul rather than lead*.

As we enter our next level of maturity, the rules of the game are changing; we are now entering a period of **thriving rather than surviving.**

Heart Power. What does heart power have to do with freedom? Historically, we operated from a consciousness of power that was founded in a habitat of survival. This created a competitive nature within us; therefore, power was ego-based. This survival environment is expressed as *me against you, us against them, inequality, and separation consciousness*.

This perpetuated a lot of fear. Power became abusive and controlling, and as a result, freedom became a commodity! This is because the foundation of our systematic structures was established in disparity, which resulted in oppression, disempowerment, enslavement, suffering, and disrespect for the value of life itself. Over time, we either gave up believing in our freedom, escaped into sleepiness, and forgot we were innately free or went into a state of *What's the point? It won't make a difference anyway*!

THE TIME FOR AWAKENING AND REMEMBERING HAS ARRIVED!

We are now on our evolutionary path to *thrive consciousness*. We are remembering who we are and awakening to our sovereignty. We are unleashing our innate right to freedom, harmony, and peace. **True freedom comes from a heart-centered place that naturally cultivates equality, respect, and dignity for all.** We are now being invited to align to this liberating power rather than an egoic-centered power.

Entering the map of our hearts, we will now explore the terrain and create the era of Unity Consciousness!

SURVIVE	THRIVE
Separation	Connection
Competition	Cooperation
Should	Resonance
Superficial	Depth
Ego	Heart
Conflict	Harmony
Power / Fear	Power / Love
I / Me	We
War	Peace

WHAT IS FREEDOM?

The actual definition of freedom is "*The power or right to act, speak, or think as one wants without hindrance or restraint. The state of not being imprisoned or enslaved. Absence of necessity, coercion, or constraint in choice.*"

WHY IS CLAIMING FREEDOM IMPORTANT?

In freedom, we have the **power of choice**! Our Soul has our Divine blueprint for this incarnation, which is communicated through our **inner resonance.**

We each have different paths here in this earth school, just like students in University or College who study various topics and themes and are at varying levels of learning, yet under the same roof. From a spiritual perspective, there isn't a right or wrong, better or worse perspective to what we are studying or our level of learning.

As we become more Soul-infused and heart-centered, it becomes easier to honor our guidance and choose from it rather than outside input.

Think of it like we are all together creating a painting. We each have our individual paintbrush and are responsible for contributing to this painting using our brush. All brushes are created equal, yet some are wider, smaller, larger, or have been dipped in different colors.

Our inner resonance guides us to where, when, and how to apply our strokes to the painting. **Without this freedom to honor our own power of choice, we will be limited or unable to contribute and experience the way our Soul wants to or has intended for its ultimate experience.**

Why Is This Important? We align to our path of highest fulfillment by following and acting from our inner resonance and heart. **Soul's blueprint is our intended purpose and potential for the current incarnation, which is expressed when we choose to honor inner resonance.**

This is how we become authentically aligned and create the life we deeply desire. **When we honor our Soul's guidance, we are brought to our highest good and the highest good for all life as well.** Thankfully, there is no right or wrong, pass or fail, or good or bad to the Soul.

The Soul transcends the polarity; however, the personality doesn't. The personality is learning to harmonize the polarity or to rise above this polarity which is where real alignment to unconditional love and freedom resides. Therefore, learning to listen to our inner resonance and honoring it is a gracious and unifying process and is part of our transformational journey! This means we can't get it wrong!!! To the Soul, it's all about learning, growing, and healing; ultimately, the Soul will only agree to an experience if it meets this criterion.

The more we understand this, the more freedom we can feel in our experiences because we can now begin to focus on the more profound meaning and gift inherent in each of our experiences. We are learning in Earth school; each experience is a *classroom*.

When we can reach a point in our process where we can seek the meaning and more profound purpose, and most importantly, the opportunity in the classroom, we can move through it faster and with much greater ease and lightness.

Polarity and Earth School. The premise of this earth school is that we learn through polarity. We learn to harmonize and transcend this dualism, both individually and as a collective. We are now at the point of our evolutionary path where we are beginning the journey of transcending the experience (*classroom*) of polarity. This predominately happens through our unique experiences and subsequent personal transformation.

There is a microcosm/macrocosm effect at play! **When we heal and evolve within ourselves, we contribute to and facilitate the transformation and healing of all life. This is why working on our personal growth, healing, and transformation is the most impactful place to begin.**

Freedom Frequency. Transforming our consciousness is an ongoing process that facilitates the opportunity of alignment to a higher vibration. **If we use our consciousness to align to a higher frequency**, our actions become more impactful in creating freedom and love rather than fear and separation.

With more awareness, we can now recognize our inner guidance and therefore choose from that cognizance. If we aren't aware we have a choice or that our choices have an effect, we live and create our lives through more of an unconscious reality and reactivity.

Once we have more awareness, we can process our emotions, like anger or fear, and then choose to align and create from a place of freedom and love.

Even With Consciousness, We Still Need To Choose Our Frequency. Although it becomes easier, it is still a choice. Just because someone has consciousness doesn't mean they are operating from a higher frequency. Someone can also be operating from a high frequency and not have more awareness.

The gift of awareness is such that we can become more of a conscious creator of what we choose to give energy to and how we choose to align. For example, imagine we see an injustice, and as a result, we become angry. If we act from this anger, we contribute to the consciousness we are trying to change because we are 'acting' from anger, creating and attracting more of the same.

We have the awareness to recognize the injustice, yet our frequency is at the level of anger. We are learning to transform the anger first, then act, creating a different outcome. This is how we disrupt the entrenched patterns, such as injustice, inequality, greed, and fear.

The anger is coming up because we hold unresolved anger, or whatever the emotional response may be, in our subconscious. Once aware of this trigger, we can begin transmuting or transforming that anger into compassion, passion, or freedom as an example.

From the new state of alignment (*compassion, freedom*), we act from a place of more impact because we operate from a higher frequency.

This is where the real impact and change we wish to see can happen, which is why as Gandhi put it, *We need to be the change we wish to see in the world!*

This is because higher frequencies negate and counterbalance lower frequencies. Think of frequency as the speed at which it vibrates. Fear and anger have more density, so they vibrate at a lower frequency or a slower vibration.

Freedom and love vibrate faster because they are less dense and therefore vibrate faster and are termed higher. It's not better or worse; it's simply how energy operates.

Energy, by its nature, seeks to be balanced, harmonized, transformed, or transmuted. Symptoms, including physical, mental, or emotional ones, are ways energy is trying to express or transform.

These energies can also be stored in our subconscious, which is why we can surprise ourselves when we behave or act beyond our conscious mind and respond strongly to a person, place, or event.

We have these responses when we have unresolved energies! They come up at these times because they are seeking resolution. For example, if we respond to something with anger, it's because we have unresolved anger that needs to be addressed.

If we are in the presence of someone grieving, and we feel their grief and hold the vibration of grief with them, we are witnessing them and can support them; however, we are holding the same frequency of grief. So, we are giving more energy to that vibration. We are much more impactful and an agent for healing when we can hold a frequency of compassion as an example. Compassion vibrates higher and is therefore facilitating an opening of a higher vibration. Grief now has an opening to transform into compassion, which, at some level, can now be accessed by the person if they so choose.

It also offers an opportunity for healing, counterbalancing the grief to a degree, and opening space for the movement of that energy. **The frequency of compassion is doing the healing; we are simply**

aligning that frequency. Which feels better than holding the space of grief, so it's a win/win!!

Collectively and individually, we were previously operating from fear, anger, frustration, limitation, jealousy, separation, and war; the predominant level of consciousness was egocentric. Therefore, there was minimal awareness or care for the impact, consequence, or ripple effect our choices and actions would create for ourselves, our species, all beings, our planet, and our future generations. If there was a consideration, it came from a *survive* mentality rather than a *thrive* mentality.

Our Soul's guidance doesn't come from or create fear or separation; therefore, when we honor our inner resonance, we are guided to align and create higher frequencies. We care about all life, and our choices will create the highest good for self and all!

Opportunity Of Learning From Polarity. How and why would we benefit from this way of learning? From a spiritual perspective, our Soul is Love. It only knows love and wants to experience and master this quality and other expressions of the quality of love.

For example, how can I understand compassion if I've never experienced suffering? How can I genuinely understand forgiveness if I've not had to forgive or sought to be forgiven? If I have not touched the depth of fear and separation, how can I genuinely touch the depth of love and connectivity more deeply?

OUR GROWTH COMES FROM EXPLORING THE DIFFERENT SHADES AND HUES.

Imagine that each quality is a color. Examples of qualities include love, freedom, peace, success, compassion, harmony, creativity, and joy….! The Soul wants to experience each quality in a deeper, more expansive way.

We may already experience and know a level of love, kindness, compassion, success, abundance, freedom…to a certain degree. Like the color blue, we know it as blue. Then we start to understand it differently, deeper, and more uniquely as it expresses in its different shades and hues of blue.

Without the backdrop of polarity, we wouldn't have the environment to explore, experience, and embody the shades of the Soul qualities. **We are learning the different shades and hues of a quality.**

Everyone here in Earth School is mastering **Love,** and we are now entering a mastery class of **Freedom**!! They are united. We are entering a new shade and depth of understanding, claiming, and rising of Freedom! How exciting!!

WHAT KEEPS US FROM CLAIMING OUR FREEDOM?

To some degree, we are all awakening to freedom. Every being has a right to be free! However, the varying degrees of intensity or experience of claiming freedom depends on the country, culture, lineage, societal structure, or familial/relationship dynamics we are dealing with.

Seek To Rise: Awareness is a potent catalyst of change; if there's a lack thereof, it can be one of our biggest obstacles! Especially to freedom. We have been conditioned and trained not to know, trust or believe in our freedom. So even if we become aware of the ways we aren't free, **we need to be willing to go within and explore and transform the reasons we aren't free.**

This often results in some type of change, which in and of itself can become a block to claiming our freedom. This is because while we yearn for change, we equally fear it. Resistance can present in many ways, consciously or subconsciously. Some main reasons are fear of loss, being judged, harmed, ostracized, abandoned, branded as

14

different, or not being loved and accepted, to name just a few.

Additional obstacles are ways we've been domesticated: our limiting beliefs, our past, our fear of the future, expectations, attachments, or our deep need to belong. There can also be projections, imprints, transferences, and inherited programming that needs to be resolved or cleared.

Let's look at an example of how a limiting belief can be an obstacle. Imagine, as a child, we experience or perceive that we were abandoned by one of our parents. That can set up a subconscious belief that it isn't safe for us to love because we will be abandoned. This creates experiences where we either attract people who fulfill that belief or perpetuate it. We may not open our hearts at all out of fear of being hurt and abandoned. Either way, we don't feel free and safe to love and be open-hearted. Therefore, we block off experiences of love that we innately desire.

So Where Do We Begin? Sometimes we can have a spontaneous awakening or healing that sets us on a path of freedom. Often, it's a blossoming that takes time, gentleness, an open heart and willingness, and yes, a bit of courage!!

Ultimately, it's a beautiful sacred journey into our hearts and Souls! A path that leads to incredible fulfillment and peace where we meet our true Sovereign Self!!

FREEDOM AS A PROCESS

There are many paths to freedom! The personal journey we navigate is indicative of what our individual Soul has chosen to study, master, and contribute. For example, one Soul may be experiencing the color blue as a deep navy shade of blue, and another Soul may be exploring a turquoise shade of blue. Let's explore how that may present in our earth school experience!

DIFFERENT ASPECTS OF FREEDOM

Freedom in Containment. For some, it could be an awakening and recognizing where we aren't free. Others may experience finding freedom in containment. An extreme example of this would be Victor Frankl's experience where he maintained mental, emotional, and Soul freedom while enduring extreme abuse as a prisoner in a Holocaust prisoner camp.

Other classrooms could include being responsible for a family while learning to find personal freedom in certain areas while maintaining that responsibility. There could also be periods of our lives of containment, such as when we are in school or dealing with a physical, financial, or mental/emotional challenge or limitation.

A beautiful way to relate to this path is to imagine a toddler yearning to explore and individuate. For safety reasons, it wouldn't be wise to let the toddler roam freely. In a specific contained space, like a fenced-in deck or yard, they could have safe, free reign to explore within the parameters of the boundaries of the fenced-in area.

Giving Freedom. We may find ourselves learning to give someone or others freedom while also learning to accept their beliefs or choices even though they differ from our own.

Freedom of Expression. Often this path has many paths within itself. That means to express ourselves freely and authentically; we need to learn to become our true authentic selves. We may go through different experiences of learning to be free from our past, cultural, familial, societal, gender, or sexual identification conditioning or abusive relationships.

We Are Learning To Accept And Claim Freedom. Recognizing and healing the ways we aren't free and choosing freedom regardless of our fears is the nature of this classroom. We may also find ourselves advocates or ambassadors of freedom. As we become more aware of freedom, we will also begin to recognize where we have also been denying freedom to others.

There are many paths to exploring freedom. The more aware we become of ourselves, the more we identify the patterns and beliefs underlying our themes or classrooms. The clearer we are, the more empowered we become because we have the awareness **to choose!**

AFFIRMATIONS

I have the power to choose.

Sovereignty (freedom) is my Divine birthright.

I am free to rise and thrive.

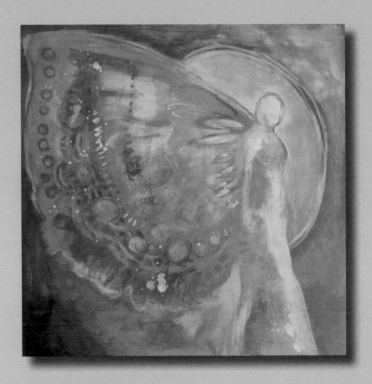

MEDITATION ~ 'I INTEND FREEDOM'

Sit in a comfortable position. Straighten the spine. Gently roll the shoulders back and down, opening the heart space. Close the eyes, bringing focus to the Third Eye, the point between the eyebrows.

Press palms together at the heart center in prayer position.

Allow anything that's going on in your world to slowly slip away. Take a couple of deep breaths in and out from the nose bringing your awareness to your breath, body, and heart space. Notice any tension, allowing it to soften and release with each exhale.

Inhale through the nose and slowly bring your arms out wide and overhead. As you bring your arms up, imagine you are drawing in healing energy and vitality from the Sun. Exhale from the mouth, placing palms downward as you bring the arms, elbows bent, down in front of your body. As you bring your arms down, imagine you are connecting to Mama Earth and grounding the energy you've just gathered into your body. (Do this 3x)

Place either hand on your heart and the other on your lower belly.

Inhale through the nose, silently repeating, *I AM LOVE*
Hold the breath in, silently repeating, *I AM (4x)*
Exhale from the mouth, silently repeating, *I AM FREE*
(Continue this for 7 mins)

To close, bring your hands back into prayer position, palms together at your heart space. Take a minute to notice how you feel. Connect to the frequency of love and freedom. Then take a moment to feel gratitude, thinking of something or someone you are thankful for. Set your intention for the remainder of your day or evening.

We are One. We are Light. We are Love. We are Free.
(Total 11 minutes. Feel free to shorten or lengthen)

INSIGHTS & JOURNALING ~ *Freedom 1,2,3*

In your own journal or on the pages to follow in this book, take some time to ponder your answers to the following questions.

1. *"Our inner resonance guides us to where, when, and how to apply our strokes to the painting. Without this freedom to honor our own power of choice, we will be limited or unable to contribute and experience the way our Soul wants to or has intended for its ultimate experience."*
   - What are your beliefs around power and freedom?
   - Are they based on *survive* or *thrive consciousness*?
   - Redefine your concept of *power* based on *thrive consciousness*.

2. *"We are unleashing our innate right to freedom, harmony, and peace.* **True freedom comes from a heart-centered place that naturally cultivates equality, respect, and dignity for all.** *We are now being invited to align to this liberating power rather than an egoic-centered power."*
   - Are you limited or have you lost freedom in any areas of your life?
   - Where do you need to reclaim or activate your power of choice?

3. *"Energy, by its nature, seeks to be balanced, harmonized, transformed, or transmuted. Symptoms, including physical, mental, or emotional ones, are ways energy is trying to express or transform. These energies can also be stored in our subconscious, which is why we can surprise ourselves when we behave or act beyond our conscious mind and respond strongly to a person, place, or event. We have these responses when we have unresolved energies! They come up at these times because they are seeking resolution."*
   - What light does it shed on your life?
   - Describe your physical, mental, and emotional responses to this notion.

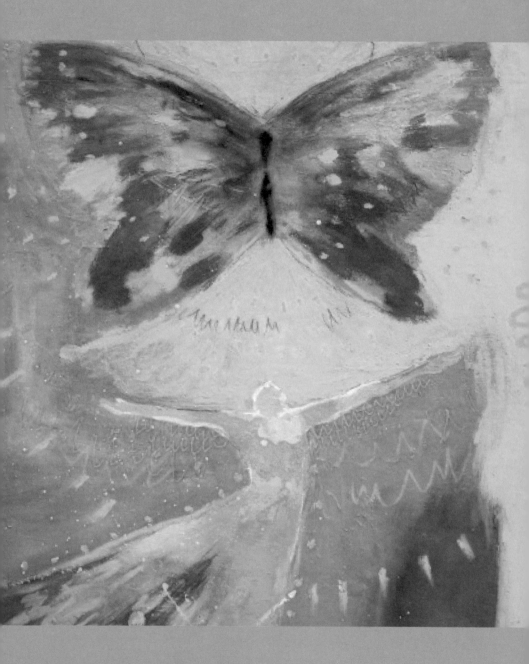

Chapter 2:

Freeing Ourselves From the Codependent Loop

"Codependency is an obstacle to Love."

Jai Dev

As we explore the complexity of finding freedom within the context of relationships more deeply, we are invited to remember that we are always seeking more love and connection on some level. All that we experience will be in some way guiding us towards that. While some paths are clear-cut, many are winding and twisting terrain; every path leads to our evolution.

FREEDOM FROM CODEPENDENCY

To truly understand freedom, we need to explore the theme of codependency. This is especially relevant now because codependency was part of the fabric of the previous paradigm of survival. As we transition into *thrive consciousness*, we are uplevelling into interdependent relationships.

Creating More Meaningful Relationships. To do this, we need to become aware of what codependency means and how it blocks freedom. When we understand and become aware of the underlying patterns that are maintaining the dynamics of our connections, we can begin to heal and shift them into more fulfilling, loving, and healthy ones. With awareness, we can start to **create a new version of ourselves** and, therefore, our alliances with others.

It is also important to remember through this process that just because we become aware that we are involved in a codependent dynamic doesn't mean it needs to end. The answer is always to begin with going inward, where all our answers genuinely lie. When we seek to understand our role in the scenario and the wounds that keep us entangled, we can begin to heal, transform and shift from within. Then, from this new space of awareness, we will know whether we are divinely meant to remain in the relationship. If we are, as we shift our inner landscape, our outer changes; therefore, our dynamics will change. And if not, then we can part ways empowered in love, kindness, and integrity.

Why Is Codependency An Obstacle To Love? At its root, codependency is founded on fear and inequality. Therefore, the heart center can't be fully opened in this dynamic. We aren't in full sovereignty or alignment with our inner resonance; we are operating in separation consciousness, which generates more fear and separation, not love. Love is free and, by its nature, creates more love, harmony, and equality. Our relationships are often our most beautiful and challenging classrooms because the catalyst for transformation is often ignited within this realm. This is why exploring freedom, or lack thereof, within the dynamics of our relationships is usually where most of our energy gravitates.

Why Is This? We tend to have more attachments, expectations, and, most importantly, projections in our relationships.

A projection is a subconscious wound that gets established during a time of trauma or pain that is too much to process or deal with and therefore bypasses the conscious mind and goes directly into the subconscious mind. Because energy, by its nature, seeks harmonization, transformation, or transmutation, it will rise and express to fulfill one of these alchemized states. When we place our negative traits or unwanted emotions onto another, like someone who bullies or puts down another for being anxious or insecure to avoid acknowledging those same tendencies within themselves, we are projecting.

Expectations are when we think something should be or go a certain way, and attachments are when we hold on to something out of fear! Usually, fear of loss and pain.

How Are Attachments Released? Attachments are the underlying wounds and pieces of ourselves we've lost or believe have been stolen along the way and we are driven to fulfill or find the fragmented parts of ourselves in another person, situation, or substance. We can only fulfill these wounds by our awareness and healing of them. Attachments are released when we begin to turn our focus inward to transform and integrate our fragments and wounds.

Attachments, expectations, and projections are all judgments, perceiving that something is good or bad, right or wrong, or pass or fail, and all stem from an underlying fear or separation consciousness.

Earth School Is A School Of Duality/Polarity. This experiential school of polarity means we are learning and mastering Soul qualities such as joy, peace, kindness, success, forgiveness, and more. In this way, we may experience the opposite, and in our transformational journey, we alchemize into a higher frequency quality. This is how we experience a quality in a more profound embodied way. The premise is that if we've never experienced suffering, and learned about compassion, then how much compassion can we give?

Embodiment. To embody a quality is to become the frequency. An example is we are not just experiencing a peaceful state; we are the frequency of peace. We literally become peace. It becomes a part of our nature, just as palpable and real as the color of our eyes or our natural height.

As we evolve and become more aware, we can grow with greater ease and gentleness. We don't require the same degree of polarity of struggle or suffering. *Yes Please!!!!*

We also become more open to downloads of understanding, which in turn accelerates our growth. This is more of the arena of *thrive consciousness*. In the previous paradigm of the survival theme, the setup was based on judgment and fear consciousness, two fundamental blocks to love and freedom.

As we become more aware of our underlying attachments and judgments, it is helpful to remain gentle and loving with ourselves. Remember that **the Soul operates from a learning, growing, and healing place.** The ego operates from right to wrong and good to bad. When we can keep returning to this, our experiences are more meaningful, and our growth happens more quickly yet gently.

As we shift from an ego-driven personality into more of a Soul-infused personality, the nature of our relationships will also be uplevelling and transforming. The foundational dynamic of this evolvement is moving away from codependency to interdependency. Codependency is based on fear, lack, and victim consciousness, which is the belief that what we are experiencing is happening to us, not for us, and that we have no choice in the matter. Underlying and maintaining this base is what's referred to as the codependent loop.

Understanding and becoming aware of the codependent loop is a significant factor in dismantling codependent relationships because of the nature of the emotions involved. Because as we begin to disrupt or change the dynamics, it may activate uncomfortable feelings. We may wonder if it's the most healthy and loving thing to do for everyone when it can feel so awful and conflicting!!!

Programming, conditioning, old training, and imprinting underlie this foundation. Knowing this during the dismantling phase can facilitate much more ease and gentleness as the changes and healing process. For example, if we are prompted to end a toxic relationship, even if we know it is the best thing for us because we are not growing or are being harmed, it can still elicit guilt or confusion about ending it. One of the most common responses is feeling bad for the person being left, which can prevent or prolong the relationship's ending.

What Is The Codependent Loop? It happens when we do something, usually for another person, because we feel we *should*, are obligated, or feel it's our duty! We may have been trained that way or are gaining something from it; this is called negative motivation. However, it's not genuinely serving our highest good, health, or sovereignty because it's a lower frequency.

Think about a child seeking attention and, when not getting it, begins to act out in a way that attracts a response such as criticism or punishment. Even though it's a limiting response, it's attention! At our core, though, our response or action is not something we want to be doing, or we are energetically, physically, mentally, emotionally harmed, or drained from doing so. In other words, it's coming from the consciousness of appeasement. This can be as simple as agreeing to go out for dinner with someone; when all we want to do is go to bed early. When we don't honor our body's guidance and appease another by agreeing to go for dinner, that registers as an incongruency and creates disharmony within us. This is a codependent response.

A more extreme example is when we remain in a situation or relationship despite abuse or inequality, and we absolutely know it is not for our highest good to stay. Yet, we do it out of extreme fear, coercion, or guilt. This is a much more complex dynamic as there could be actual abuse or extreme manipulation activated or threatened upon dismantling this dynamic. In this case, solid support, thought, and care is needed.

Operating From Appeasement. When we think or act from a place of *I should* or ***What should I do?*** we generally operate from domestication, which is how we've been conditioned and trained to operate from expectations, fear of judgments, and fulfilling the needs of others rather than operating from a place of inner resonance. This creates inner conflict and incongruency, and it never feels good in the long run!!!

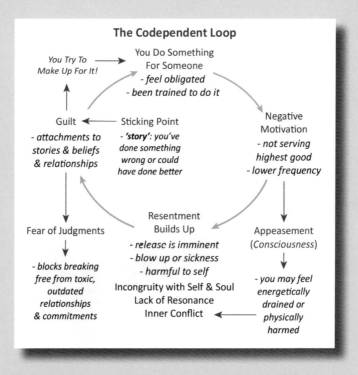

The Codependent Loop

You Try To Make Up For It! → You Do Something For Someone
- *feel obligated*
- *been trained to do it*

Guilt ← Sticking Point
- *attachments to stories & beliefs & relationships*
- *'story': you've done something wrong or could have done better*

Negative Motivation
- *not serving highest good*
- *lower frequency*

Fear of Judgments
- *blocks breaking free from toxic, outdated relationships & commitments*

Resentment Builds Up
- *release is imminent*
- *blow up or sickness*
- *harmful to self*
Incongruity with Self & Soul
Lack of Resonance
Inner Conflict ←

Appeasement (*Consciousness*)
- *you may feel energetically drained or physically harmed*

Codependent Loop. *Appeasement... Resentment... Release/Expression... Guilt... Appeasement*

Here Is The Pattern. We choose or act from appeasement. This creates inner disharmony, and resentment builds. The resulting energy then needs to be released, which is usually expressed in some form of blow-up towards self or others. This then creates a feeling of guilt. And once guilt and the feeling of having done something wrong kicks in, appeasement rearises to eliminate the sense of guilt. **The guilt is usually the sticking point of dismantling codependency because of the deep feeling that we've done something wrong and need to atone!**

Attachments and judgments, especially fear of judgments, are the main blocks from breaking free of toxic, unhealthy, abusive, or outdated relationships, patterns, and behaviors. As social beings, it is innate for us to want to create connections. The difference with an attachment is there's an underlying fear of loss, pain, change, or avoidance. Therefore, this is the consciousness underlying the relationship and blocks love and more profound, meaningful life-giving experiences. Sometimes just becoming aware of the attachment is enough to release it energetically. And other times, we may need to explore it further for deeper understanding which may be required for transformation, or it may need to be processed through the body. We may need to *feel it to heal it*!

PROCESSING EMOTIONS

When we don't move our emotions, they build up in our subconscious or body, like a pressure cooker. Part of our process towards experiencing more love, joy, freedom, or any higher vibration is to make space for them to anchor and to create new neurological pathways.

It isn't easy, to face, lean into, and allow our emotions to flush out. It can be downright frightening. We may have also been conditioned to believe that emotions are a sign of weakness, which adds to even more suppression.

Emotions are simply **Energy in Motion.** Although it certainly

27

doesn't feel that straightforward. This is because we have memories, fear, or trauma associated with lower frequency emotions. They also are just downright uncomfortable, so we tend to do anything to avoid them. We become masters at escaping or distracting ourselves. We become adept with creative diversions to prevent or numb the rising of these painful emotions. While addictions are complex, this is an aspect of how we may become dependent on people, working, things and substances.

Sometimes we need to understand the underlying cause; however, because most of these are rooted in the subconscious, it's not necessarily relevant to always know why we are feeling what we are feeling. Sometimes too much talking or exploring about it can further embed it into the subconscious.

We keep adding more fuel to the fire rather than processing and moving the energies. Our left brain also wants to narrate what we are experiencing so it can make some logical sense to it. This can deter the movement and prolong and halt our healing and transformation.

Often, when we allow ourselves to **breathe what we feel,** if we do need to be aware of something to heal or disrupt a pattern, it arises organically and gently, especially once we've become accustomed to perceiving all that arises as an opportunity for growth or healing.

MASTER YOUR REALITY, SIT WITH THE PAIN

A beautiful way to get comfortable with our emotions is to imagine them as water or air. When an emotion arises, we can tune into the signature of it, questioning if it is anger, grief, fear, or sadness. Where do we feel it in the body? Then we can soften the body and allow it to be there. We may be at this stage for a while because we may have a lot of experience suppressing or resisting. Or perhaps it may be so intense we need to take baby steps. When we feel ready for the next stage, we lean into it and gently move towards it. It's helpful if we can also be open to the concept that what is arising isn't our enemy. It isn't against us nor trying to annihilate us. It's just energy in motion. This creates space, and we don't feel so personalized with it. We feel safe.

As we move towards it, it will usually start to rise. This can again cause us to want to retreat, so here we may need to relax again and allow it. When ready, imagine the energy like a wave; as it rises, visualize, feel, or hear it as a giant wave. We want to keep breathing into it. If it feels too much at any time, we always want to give ourselves permission to pull out and redirect. Having something to redirect to before beginning this exercise can also be helpful. It can be an affirmation such as *I am safe*, a plant in the room, or a glass of water. We have a high percentage of water in our body, from 60-75%, so drinking water is a beneficial facilitator to moving energy through the body. Water also represents emotions, so anytime we use water to facilitate the processing of emotions, it brings more ease and calm to the experience.

When able, we want to ride the wave to its peak. It will then begin to descend, and you can roll with it like a wave meeting the shore and dissolving. At this point, we will feel relief or even the entire space open if it has been fully transmuted.

Some energies take some time to dissipate entirely. Some are complete with one flow through this process. It's important we go at our own pace and never force. And keep in mind this is only a guide on processing. Everyone is different; some feel more or don't feel at all yet are aware of a sensation or restlessness. It's about finding our rhythm with this and following our inner guidance!

Some things are meant to unfold in layers. When we do need to do it bit by bit, we pick up from where we left off. If we haven't been able to move past the first stage, the next time we approach the energy, we are not starting from scratch. Even though, at first, it may feel like we are. As we become more comfortable with this practice, we tend to move through things faster. It becomes easier and gentler.

STEPS TO PROCESSING EMOTIONS

1. Allow and soften. Breathe to feel.

2. Lean into the emotion.

3. Let the wave rise and break.

4. Keep breathing into it and redirect if needed.

5. Roll with it to the shore

6. Breathe and tune into the relief or space that has opened.

7. Choose and intend how you will fill this space. I.E. *Love, peace, freedom…*

8. Set an intention for the rest of your day. I.E. *I intend ease and flow…*

9. Give yourself credit for courageously processing the emotion.

Other powerful ways to move energy are dancing, being in nature, cleansing, purging, or organizing. Setting an intention and then engaging in action can be enough. An example is before watching a movie or going on a walk, set the intention to process an emotion while watching the movie or on the walk. Then simply be completely present in the movie or walk.

The more we know ourselves, the easier it becomes to know what we need. The key is to keep practicing tuning into and honoring our inner resonance.

INTERDEPENDENCY

Ultimately, there is a need underlying a codependent relationship, whether with people, things, or substances. We are looking to fill a void, ease pain or recall back an aspect of ourselves we feel we've lost or has been taken from us. We are seeking outside ourselves for that fulfillment or relief.

The game changer is when we understand that our true path to wholeness comes from within. Nothing *out there* can genuinely fill a void. Not in the long run. When we begin to turn inward, whether that is processing our emotions or following more of our inner guidance, we start to experience a sense of peace and inner strength that becomes our new foundation. From here, true freedom becomes accessible.

In an interdependent relationship, we don't need another to save or fulfill anything. We are empowered knowing we have that ability within ourselves. Therefore, we are free to support another in their process, and they can help us in ours without needing to save, fix and rescue or be saved, fixed, and rescued. We understand that it is our responsibility to fill our cup, and the same goes for others. We can show up for ourselves and others with genuine heart-centered support, harmony, unity, and love. We are then enhanced and honored by another's presence in our lives, yet our happiness, peace, or lovability isn't based on or determined by another or anything outside ourselves. That is cultivated from within. We then are aligned to that frequency from within, which means we will also be attracting more of the same. *Law of similars! Like attracts like!*

This then brings deep meaning and depth to our relationships and experiences rather than depleting another by needing something from them that they ultimately cannot give us or being depleted by someone else needing something from us. **True strength and freedom don't dominate or manipulate.**

Spiritual power is a gift born of sacred love, wisdom, and grace. This is the seat of our sovereignty and our true power. This is the foundation of an interdependent relationship.

AFFIRMATIONS

I am love.

I bless and release that which no longer serves me.

I allow myself to feel to heal.

MEDITATION ~ 'I INTEND SELF LOVE'

Lie on your back in a comfortable position. Bring your legs into a **V** position, relaxing your arms to your sides, about 3-6 inches away from your body, palms facing upward.

Imagine you are in a gentle, healing, protective cocoon of light. Take a couple of deep breaths in through the nose, exhaling from the mouth, releasing any heaviness, tension, or stress. Do this 3-5x. Then relax the breath, allowing it to be in its natural rhythm.

Set an intention to release any energies that aren't yours, that are no longer serving you, or that are ready to be cleared and released and that any negative cords, attachments, projections, or energetic drains are cut, cleared, and dissipated.

Set an intention to replace what is released with the quality of self-love. To be filled with gentle, nurturing, comforting, and loving energies. To feel hopeful, optimistic, and light.

Bring your focus to your lower body (feet, ankles, lower legs, knees, upper legs, hips, and butt). Inhale through the nose, hold the breath in and squeeze your lower body. Hold for a few seconds, then exhale from the mouth, releasing any tension stored in the lower body.

Bring your focus on your middle/upper body (lower back, lower belly, middle back, stomach, upper back, chest, hands, wrists, lower arms, elbows, upper arms, shoulders, neck, head, and face). Inhale through the nose, hold the breath in and squeeze your middle/upper body. Hold for a few seconds, then exhale from the mouth, releasing any tension stored in the middle/upper body.

Take a deep breath in, hold and squeeze your whole body for a few seconds, then exhale from the mouth, releasing the tension. Silently repeat *I AM RELAXED* (3X)

Letting go now, allow yourself to go into deep relaxation for 7 minutes.

Slowly begin to bring gentle movement into your hands, feet, and then your body, Taking a couple of deep breaths in and out. Slowly make your way up to a seated position. Set an intention for the rest of your day, evening, or sleep.

We are One. We are Light. We are Love. We are Free.
(Total 11 minutes. Feel free to shorten or lengthen)

INSIGHTS & JOURNALING ~ *Freedom 1,2,3*

In your own journal or on the pages to follow in this book, take some time to ponder your answers to the following questions.

1. *"**Why Is Codependency An Obstacle To Love?** At its root, codependency is founded on fear and inequality. Therefore, the heart center can't be fully opened in this dynamic. We aren't in full sovereignty or alignment with our inner resonance; we are operating in separation consciousness, which generates more fear and separation, not love. Love is free and, by its nature, creates more love, harmony, and equality. Our relationships are often our most beautiful and challenging classrooms because the catalyst for transformation is often ignited within this realm. This is why exploring freedom, or lack thereof, within the dynamics of our relationships is usually where most of our energy gravitates."*

    • Can you recognize when your heart is closed or when you are shutting down?

    • How can you begin to feel safe opening your heart, shining your light and expressing yourself?

2. *"As we shift from an ego-driven personality into more of a Soul-infused personality, the nature of our relationships will also be uplevelling and transforming. The foundational dynamic of this evolvement is moving away from codependency to interdependency. Codependency is based on fear, lack, and victim consciousness, which is the belief that what we are experiencing is happening to us, not for us, and that we have no choice in the matter. Underlying and maintaining this base is what's referred to as the codependent loop."*

    • What do you fear?

    • What would you like to experience more often in your relationships, including your relationship with yourself?

    • Can you identify where you are operating from fear, attachment or expectation?

3. ***"What Is The Codependent Loop?*** *It happens when we do something, usually for another person, because we feel we should, are obligated, or feel it's our duty! We may have been trained that way or are gaining something from it; this is called negative motivation. However, it's not genuinely serving our highest good, health, or sovereignty because it's a lower frequency."*

- **"SHOULD DETOX"**
- For a day or a week, notice where you are operating from a premise of "**should**". Journal insights and awarenesses from this experience.
    - Should I go to the party?
    - Should I wear that dress?
    - I shouldn't have said or done that
    - I should call my _____
    - I should lose some weight

Chapter 3:

Uncovering Potential and Possibilities: Releasing Our Narratives

"I can choose either to be a victim of the world or an adventurer in search of treasure. It's all a question of how I view my life."

Paulo Coelho

NARRATIVES

In the previous paradigm setup, we operated from survival-ego-dominated consciousness and identified and created everything through our stories. Our narratives are the beliefs we tell ourselves or have been told to believe. They are predominantly subconscious and can be inherited from the collective, our ancestral lineage, our culture, and our experiences. Another way to view this is to see this as our programming.

Earth School Is Unique. This is an experiential school, which is why it makes such a fertile landscape for learning, growing, and healing. We have programs inherent to attract and create specific experiences. Some of these are common to everyone who incarnates here, similar to every student at a particular university who must fulfill specific requirements to graduate from that school. Other programming is unique to everyone based on our own Soul's itinerary.

There are 86 Soul qualities, one of which is **Love.** We are all mastering love here in Earth school, which is why there has been so much fear; it is the opposite of love. Our Soul will also be working on other Soul qualities too, such as creativity, success, faith, self-worth, forgiveness, and more. Additional soul qualities are listed in *references.*

Our Soul chooses our programming based on the qualities intended for our incarnational blueprint. We may continue or deepen those we have already studied and concentrate on new ones.

The more we heal and evolve in consciousness, different programming gets activated. This can also occur when we reach a specific age or encounter a particular person or place.

Another facet of our programming is based on unresolved energies or incomplete learning the Soul has been seeking. Our Soul is on a continuum, meaning it may take many incarnations to grow and heal something. To the Soul, each incarnation is like a page out of a chapter of a book. The Soul will also want a myriad of experiences to bring mastery to the qualities being studied. For example, if we are mastering forgiveness, we will want to experience being forgiven and having to forgive.

UNRESOLVED ENERGIES

While we may, at some level, agree with the experience we are having; this earth school is no joke. It can be an extraordinarily intense and harsh climate. In fact, it's considered the "Harvard" of schools because of its fierceness and hardness. It is also said that those who incarnate here are truly courageous Souls. The gift in this school is what we gain from being here equals our experiences. We deeply acquire growth and understanding, unlike what we could achieve elsewhere. As Kyron says, 'All beings from across the galaxies will recognize our courageous Souls by the unique colors we've acquired by choosing to be a part of this earth experience.'

With all this in mind, when we do have an experience, the energies must be processed through the personality. Because energy seeks to be transformed or transmuted, it will continue to run from lifetime to lifetime until that happens. This process is the actual alchemy of how the transformation occurs. Through this process, we become aware of something we weren't before. For example, if we have been disappointed countless times by our loved ones not being able to support us in crucial times, this could create doubt. We may even feel this with Spirit. Through this experience of doubt, we are faced with questioning and redefining what faith is to us, whether faith in ourselves, others, or the Universe. We may be in doubt for many years or lifetimes until we begin to see events from a different perspective. When we do, the energy starts to move, shift and transform. We may become more open to faith and discover a new or renewed sense of faith. This came to be through the occurrence of doubt. We can then begin to transcend the dramas and traumas that created doubt.

When we transform and evolve, a new version of ourselves can express and come through. New versions of others can come through too, which is how our reality and relationships can shift by simply working on our inner selves.

THE CLASSROOM

All the traumas, dramas, and events we experience play out in what can be referred to as a classroom. Playground or any other interpretation can also be used here, depending on one's inner resonance. It is helpful to remember that there is a container where the opportunity to learn and grow happens. Each relationship, event, and state of being, such as depression, grief, or illness, are all examples of a classroom.

Some of our classrooms are individualized; some are wider, such as the culture or country we are born in, the cohort or generation we are a part of, or the collective itself. Understanding this can be completely perspective changing because we can become more objective about what is occurring. A common response we have while in an experience is to resist it. This prolongs the experience and can create blocks and obstacles to the growth and learning that the circumstance offers.

Instead of being caught up in the experience or classroom, we can view it as the container it is and begin to ask **why the classroom is presenting.** Seeking the meaning and purpose makes us available to the awareness needed. We maintain empowerment because we are **choosing** to focus on what is ready for healing and transformation, which is the point of the classroom in the first place.

Even in the depth of pain, and even if we still truly wish it wasn't happening, we can begin to accept and seek the opportunity the classroom offers, for there is always a gift in every experience.

This awareness also allows the opportunity to perceive that what is happening is **for us, not to us,** shifting us out of victim consciousness. This is where the real magic can begin. We can connect deeper with our Soul and strengthen our faith that our Soul is guiding us to a higher aspect of ourselves. As a result, we begin to trust ourselves and the process more. This also accelerates the learning because we aren't resisting and prolonging. By being open to the *why,* the energy can move, and the answers can come forth. Sometimes this is all that's needed to complete the classroom. If the energy remains, it's because there is still something for us to learn or grow from. Some classrooms are quick, others last for years, and some may be lifelong themes.

STEPS TO APPROACHING THE CLASSROOM

The key is first to recognize the situation as a classroom. Then to be open to the meaning and purpose. Thirdly, go to the energy signature presenting, which could be conflict, grief, loss, betrayal or otherwise. Then we can begin to process or move these energies.

The benefit of pursuing the energy is that we are not adding fuel to the fire. Knowing that energy must be converted brings our focus on processing rather than giving it more undue attention. An example is if we are triggered with anger, we begin to give our attention to the anger by focusing on the *why, who, or what* happened that caused the anger. Say we get cut off by someone in traffic, and we become infuriated. We start sending that person nasty thoughts and keep going over the scenario in our minds. Then we get home and start talking about what happened; it stirs up the anger again and maybe even fuels it more. This also leaks our power, so at a deeper level, we become hijacked by the situation, the classroom. This causes us to get caught up in the classroom or the story rather than the energy signature.

If we step back and go directly to what was set off for us, in this case, anger, and we can recognize that we have responded in anger because we have that running unresolved in our subconscious, then we won't be caught up in the classroom. We can then begin to move the emotion of anger. We understand the 'why 'of the classroom being presented. We can be aware or open to the notion that we have attracted that situation on some level, or it wouldn't have presented itself to us. This is also how we learn to read our environment. So much of what we are vibrating out of our subconscious is beyond our conscious mind; therefore, when we approach what is *presenting* in our outer world as a reflection or a mirror, we can quickly rectify and shift that which we no longer want to be experiencing.

41

To recapitulate this example:

- **Classroom/Circumstance** – A person cut us off

- **Classroom Theme** – The healing of anger

- **Opportunity** – Neutrality, peace, or calm

- **Outcome** – 100% responsibility for response, acceptance that we attracted this experience to serve our Soul, not to punish us

- **Gift** – We stay out of victimhood and are open to claiming our freedom

By responding this way, we have also stayed out of victim consciousness, one of our biggest openings to claiming our freedom. We've done so by taking responsibility that we have attracted this on some level to serve us, not punish us.

This may also open us to more love and compassion as we may also be able to see it from another's perspective. In the case of our example, we might become aware that the person who cut us off may have been in a hurry to the hospital to be with a loved one. Who knows!!! And while we don't need to know the details of the *other story*, we can be open to more compassion than conflict. At the minimum, we are neutral. Most importantly, we have been able to keep the focus on ourselves and heal the anger.

Opening space facilitates freedom. When we approach life this way, we become *freer, more inspired, loving, aware, and peaceful*. This is because we are opening space for these frequencies. It's like having a closet full of old clothes that no longer fit or resonate with us. To make room for the new clothes we want to put in our closet, we must clear the old clothes first.

We also free ourselves up to be of more impactful service to others.

It takes a lot of energy to maintain conflict and lower frequencies. It truly is a gift of kindness to self and others to turn inward and process our emotions because, over time, through this process, we have the opportunity to become more loving, joyful, and light.

REWRITING OUR STORIES

The greatest illusion is the illusion of separation. Until we disrupt our old stories like *I'm not good enough, I don't deserve abundance, or things will never change because…*, we will continue to create more fear, suffering, and struggle for ourselves and others. That's because we were operating from a foundational program of suffering and limitation in survival consciousness. Most of our old stories are founded in this mirage. Separation is based on fear consciousness which sustains judgment. If we perceive something as good/bad or right/wrong, then we are in judgment, which creates more of the idea that we are disconnected. We will then fear others, life, or opening our hearts. And then we will create and attract more of that.

By recognizing that this is just a story we are telling ourselves or have been taught to believe, we can begin to ask ourselves what we want to believe, what we want our new stories to be, for ourselves, humanity, Mama earth, and our future generations.

It's helpful to remember that when we become clear and intentional about what we want to create, anything that could prevent this may come up to be released.

For example, we become aware that we want deeper and more meaningful love in our relationships. If we have unresolved energies or programming of not feeling worthy of love, jealousy, or betrayal, these will rise to be alchemized.

This occurs because we are ready for something new. Therefore, anything old or blocking this must be released to open space to allow this process. The challenge is that there is a high probability we won't recognize that what is coming up for healing directly relates to our intention. It's arising so we create and receive what we are intending. A beautiful way to remind and support ourselves that this may occur is to set up prompts or write them down somewhere visible.

Our freedom rising is accessing our birthright to create our reality. We have always been creating, just predominantly in an unconscious way. Activating our creatorship aligns us to *thrive consciousness*, and we begin to transcend the polarity of separation consciousness.

Imagine we are the writer, director, producer, and most importantly, the main **star** of our show; what would we choose to experience and create? Doesn't this process feel more fun, free, and joyful? We can genuinely start to let our light **shine!** In the words of Nelson Mandela, **"As we let our own light shine, we unconsciously give other people permission to do the same."** Our authentic journey within always serves the highest and greatest good for all!

WE ARE ALWAYS EXPERIENCING OURSELVES

As part of the survival setup, we were trained and conditioned to compare ourselves and our classrooms to others or to feel defeated or less than if others around us weren't experiencing the same challenges or traumas. One of the most emancipating paths is learning to stay focused on our own classrooms and in our own lanes.

There is a sophisticated choreography underlying our experiences, meaning we will constantly interact with other Souls, fulfilling Soul agreements and, to a degree, merging with other people's stories. The more Soul-infused we become, the more we learn to leverage negativity and discern what is ours and what isn't. This in and of itself can be a gift of freedom that words cannot convey. Instead of trying to keep up or be like others, we recognize and align to the sacredness and purpose of our life path. We can genuinely view all experiences as opportunities to upgrade and uplevel, which brings us a more profound sense of purpose, fulfillment, peace, and ability to be in the present moment, where our true power to create our intentions resides.

Suppose we have experienced significantly more pain or trauma than others, which is relative. In that case, a common rebuttal is that it's easy to say we forgive if we've never really been betrayed, or it's easy to be positive if there's never been a significant loss, restriction, or injustice experienced. When we can focus and come to trust our Soul's path, regardless of whether other people understand our lives and classrooms, we no longer desire to give attention or care to that. We are free to *live and let live.* To be fully enriched by our unique journey opens us to extracting our fullest potential and expression.

AFFIRMATIONS

I am courageous and I choose to grow from all experiences.

I am a creator and can rewrite my stories.

I trust my inner resonance.

MEDITATION ~ 'I INTEND TRANSFORMATION'

Sit in a comfortable seated position. Straighten the spine. Gently roll the shoulders back and down, opening the heart space. Close the eyes bringing the focus to the Third Eye, the point between the eyebrows.

Place your left hand on your heart and your right hand over your left.

Slowly begin to inhale through the nose, noticing the breath cool as it enters the nostrils. Slowly exhale from the nose, noticing the breath warm as it leaves the nostrils. Continue for a few breaths, bringing your focus inward, releasing anything that's going on with your life.

Set an intention for gentle transformation. That on each inhale, you'll be drawing in life-giving, healing prana. On every exhale, you are releasing what no longer serves your highest good.

Inhale slowly through the nose and hold your breath in as long as you comfortably can. Exhale slowly through the nose, holding your breath out as long as you comfortably can.

Continue this rhythm of breathing. (7 mins)

(If you feel your mind wandering, gently bring it back to the focus of the breath. You can also silently repeat on the inhale that you are drawing in healing energy and on the exhale that you are releasing what no longer serves.)

Sit silently for a few moments. Noticing how you feel, allowing the energy to circulate and assimilate.

Bring palms together at the heart center in prayer position. Set your intention for the remainder of your day or evening.

We are One. We are Light. We are Love. We are Free.

(Total 11 minutes. Feel free to shorten or lengthen)

INSIGHTS & JOURNALING ~ *Freedom 1,2,3*

In your own journal or on the pages to follow in this book, take some time to ponder your answers to the following questions.

1. *"Instead of being caught up in the experience or classroom, we can view it as the container it is and begin to ask why the classroom is presenting. Seeking the meaning and purpose makes us available to the awareness needed. We maintain empowerment because we are choosing to focus on what is ready for healing and transformation, which is the point of the classroom in the first place."*
   - What classrooms and repeating lessons can you recognize in your life?
   - What comes up for you as you go through each one?
   - What qualities are you mastering?

2. *"The greatest illusion is the illusion of separation. Until we disrupt our old stories like I'm not good enough, I don't deserve abundance, or things will never change because…, we will continue to create more fear, suffering, and struggle for ourselves and others."*
   - What are your beliefs about what you are worthy of and deserve?
   - Create a list of your current positive life-giving habits and patterns.

3. *"Imagine we are the writer, director, producer, and most importantly, the main **star** of our show; what would we choose to experience and create? Doesn't this process feel more fun, free, and joyful? We can genuinely start to let our light **shine!**"*
   - Begin with your end in mind… Pick any future moment and create a desired vision for yourself and your life at that time.
   - Create a list of qualities you already have (5-50). For example, kind, creative, funny, strong, joyful…
   - Do you fear coming into your highest version of *self?*

Chapter 4:

Discovering Our Relationship With Self-Worth & Self-Esteem

"I shall search my Soul for the lion inside of me."

Van Morrison

WE ARE THE POWER AND PRESENCE OF THE DIVINE

Moving into this next chapter of *thrive consciousness* also means awakening to our true, Divine nature. It is time to remember and activate our sovereign selves, which is to ignite and claim our creatorship.

What exactly does this mean? The premise that we are born from the Ultimate Creator means we also have the power to create. We are an individuated spark from the Ultimate Creator or Source Energy and are here in this earth school to create, create, create! To be clear, creating doesn't just include art, music, or more; it is the power to create our realities, lives, and experiences.

The Ocean and the Cup. A Buddhist example explaining us as sparks of the Divine is the analogy of the cup from the ocean. The ocean represents Source. If we take a cup of water out of the ocean, the cup contains the essence of the water from the ocean. We, as individuals, represent the cup. We are unique individuals yet contain the Divine within, like the water in the cup.

We have always had the Divine Presence within us; however, because of the previous level of consciousness on the planet and of the human species, there hasn't been full awareness of this or of what that implies.

Our evolutionary maturation is an awakening to becoming the conscious creators and cocreators we are designed to be. We claim this when we understand that we have the power and ability to create our experiences within ourselves.

WHY OUR TRANSFORMATIONAL PROCESS IS SO IMPORTANT

We have been operating from a more ego-driven landscape, and as a result, we have been trained and conditioned to compete with each other. Survival of the fittest was paramount and ensured our survival. The repercussions of this prompted us to compare and tear each other down. Existing from this separation platform has spawned ruthless tyranny, greed, and lack of respect. It has devalued all life and beings to a critical point that many have no care or ability to perceive or feel empathy, compassion, and genuine kindness. We don't have to look very far in our history to see the pervasiveness and the cold, heart-wrenching consequences and impact of this. If we are free, yet another is not; are we yet genuinely free? Poignant words said by Nelson Mandela, **"For to be free is not merely to cast off one's chains, but to live in a way that respects and enhances the freedom of others."**

The initiation of this arises from within through our unique process of healing our internal conflicts. By redefining and shifting our beliefs and perceptions to caring and connecting deeper, first within ourselves and our relationship to self, then outward to all life, all beings, we have an impact. These shifts matter and have power because we matter! Because all life matters!

Imagine that the flapping of a butterfly's wings in one part of the world can cause a hurricane on the other side of the globe. This is considered the **Butterfly Effect**, where an action or change that doesn't seem important has a huge effect, especially in other places or around the world. It is based on the chaos theory, which states that even slight imbalances in starting conditions can lead to substantial final variations in the outcome because of the system's fundamental instability. **Or perhaps we are intricately and subtly connected in ways we are just beginning to be capable of understanding.**

There is a physics to consciousness, meaning in very simple terms that as we become more aware, our ability to see what we could previously not becomes present to us. Intelligence without consciousness will only be able to perceive to the degree of one's level of awareness.

Consider some of the innovative work and findings by Drs. Bruce Lipton, Gregg Braden, Joe Dispenza, and Nassim Haramein, to name just a few. From expanded consciousness, they are unearthing *a deeper understanding of human reality based on expanded discoveries in quantum physics, biology, and geology that will have tremendous consequences on the wellness and health of all societies.*

Imagine our level of awareness gives us the ability to see navy blue. Now imagine our awareness has expanded, and we can see two more shades of blue, an indigo blue and an aquamarine blue. Previously we only had the capacity to see navy blue. The other shades were always there, yet we couldn't access them. As our consciousness expands, we can see the other shades.

This presents the importance of seeking within and connecting to the innate power our transformational process attributes us. The more we evolve and expand our awareness, the more discerning we will be about the solutions needed to heal our world. To create more balance, equality, and freedom. Our future generations are counting on it.

THE EGO TEETER-TOTTER

While the Soul is infinite and exists beyond time and space, the ego operates in a limited and finite manner. Therefore, when it's not serving the heart and Soul, it only knows two switches: **Superiority and Inferiority.**

When superiority is activated, we feel we are better than or above others. This establishes the foundation of authoritarianism and the depreciation of others' worth, fostering inferiority, where we believe we are less than or worthless. This teeter-totter is the bedrock of codependency and is our main block to our sovereignty. Most importantly, it creates, cultivates, and sustains the beliefs that maintain separation, fear, inequality, and victim consciousness.

Loss of Power. Energy Leaks. Our beliefs shape, create, and attract our experiences, hence our realities. One result of the ego teeter-totter is that it has cultivated inherent beliefs that have diminished our self-esteem and self-worth. Our energy decreases when we give attention to anything outside us that creates a drain, imbalance, or inequality. We lose our power through our belief systems. By changing them, we reclaim our power. As Dr. Wayne Dyer articulated, *when we change the way we look at things, the things we look at change.*

THE CONNECTION BETWEEN OUR SELF-ESTEEM AND SELF WORTH

While these two Soul qualities have unique essences and features, they are intricately connected. Our self-worth cannot exceed the level and degree of our self-esteem. They are also the fundamental shapers underlying our beliefs and the version of ourselves we experience. As Paulo Coelho expressed, *we are what we believe ourselves to believe.*

Self Esteem is what we believe **about** ourselves, our attributes, and our capabilities. The opinions, perceptions, and often harsh judgments we hold on ourselves also dictate the degree of self-respect we have for ourselves. If it is too low, we will feel below average and inferior. If it is inflated, we operate from the opinion we are above average and superior. Both are judgments that create separation, limitation, fear, and disconnection.

Healthy and positive self-esteem births when we become more in tune with our true essence, **Our Soul Self**. When we are connected to who we truly are and remember, we contain the Source Energy of all Creation within us! From this understanding of unity, we can come to love and accept ourselves without judgment or comparison, and our inner compass can guide us because we know and trust ourselves.

The main pitfalls of being caught up in the superior/inferior dynamic are that it's exhausting to sustain and requires outer approval or acceptance to maintain superiority or rise out of inferiority. When we transcend this polarized dichotomy, we understand that what we seek can only come from within, from our Soul's guidance.

Imagine five people are asking us to do the same task. If we are not Soul connected, we will usually want to please whoever asks us for this task. We do this to gain something, such as acceptance, recognition, status, safety, security, or love, because something that we feel, at some level, is lacking within ourselves. The obstacle is that each person asking us to complete the task will have their versions of success upon this completion because each person is operating from their perceptions, views, and opinions. Therefore, it will, in most cases, be impossible to please each person. This may further deflate our self-esteem and is, to a more painful degree, leaking our energy. This is because we are basing the outcome on how we feel or are striving to feel something outside ourselves.

When we can release our attachments to what others think, we are cultivating freedom and inner harmony. We feel peaceful and fulfilled when we know ourselves and can operate from a place of inner resonance. Others may not understand or agree with us or our choices, yet we can feel acceptance of this. We can *live and let live*. Most importantly, we cultivate *sacred self-respect*. We can honor all aspects of ourselves, including our wounds, vulnerabilities, differences, and quirks. We begin to develop inner peace and unshakeable self-love. We can then authentically show up for others from this space. This is our path of wholeness.

Self-worth is our perceived value and often translates to how deserving we deem we are. How 'good enough' we feel. The unique balancing act with this quality is to know our worth yet maintain humility. When we are in too much humility, we won't recognize our value or receive our highest good because we will feel we aren't worthy to receive it on some level. This is a rejection of the inherent Divine Presence within us. The other extreme is having no sense of humility, where arrogant pridefulness presides. These expressions prevent us from experiencing the love, abundance, joy, and peace which are our birthrights and the nature of our true essence. We are here in human form to remember, claim and express this.

We are here to bring our Soul's brilliance forth! To understand our place in the universe's grand scheme, imagine that we are like a grain of sand while simultaneously knowing that we are glorious treasures because we are beautifully vulnerable in our humanity and Divine in our essence.

Another expression of not feeling good enough can be perfectionism, a setup for discouragement and disappointment. Here we come from a place of lack, like chasing an elusive carrot. We can never fully arrive, feel fulfilled or get it just right. Which then propagates more reason to feel and prove to ourselves that we don't have what it takes.

Our opportunity with this is to maintain a **spirit of excellence**. Knowing we are doing the best we can and approaching things from the perspective of refinement and completion rather than striving for an unrealistic and discriminating precision. We step out of perfectionism when we commit to knowing ourselves and being *real and authentic,* allowing ourselves to be in the process and **trust our journey of becoming!**

The Spiral. There is poetry to our lives. A sophisticated, intricate choreography to everything. To all our experiences, relations, and encounters. The Soul learns, grows, and heals on a spiral. This means we will always be learning, growing, and expanding. Keeping this in mind supports the journey rather than the emphasis on the destination.

Each rung on the spiral is a level of learning. Each level is a stepping stone preparing us for the next level. The previous level becomes the foundation for the next. Think of a rung on the spiral as our classroom theme, which may last for days, months, or years. The length can depend on the level of mastery the Soul seeks, and how cooperative we are to being in the flow of the experience we are having.

Imagine we are experiencing a period of significant anxiety where we are being physically affected with frightening panic attacks that present as an inability to catch the breath and rapid bounding heart palpitations. Fear of losing control or being embarrassed sets in, which leads to pulling away from being in public places or social gatherings. The people closest to us may not understand what's happening, and we begin to feel more lost, alone, and unsupported.

Now imagine we begin to get open and curious about what's happening. This may take many weeks or even years to get to this point. Learning how to hold gentle, loving space for ourselves during this process will significantly be part of our growth and evolution. There are many layers of judgment response to unravel within ourselves.

Once we get to a place where we can start seeking deeper meaning and opportunity, our experience can shift. The answers we seek start to present; perhaps a book or song comes our way, providing us with an understanding of our experience, or we have an unexpected conversation that really hits home and brings comfort and inspiration.

In this scenario, with the anxiety, we may become aware that our thoughts are constantly focused on fear of the future. We realize we are never really relaxed and in the present moment. As we explore further, we discover we hold deep beliefs that we aren't safe in the world.

Through some of the more isolated times we experienced in this state, we realized we are sensitive and take on the energies of others and the world. We recognize this about ourselves and know we need to develop tools and self-care activities to support our well-being.

The choreography is that each person we were interconnected with through this process would be in their own classroom with this experience. We may be learning more of the qualities of supporting, understanding, and loving self. While the people interacting with us may be learning to support others or to be patient, for example.

This would be the underlying Soul agreements we have made with each other. This is how our programming interconnects with each other and how we facilitate each other's growth. Regardless of the role we are playing out, we are always both giving and receiving on some level. In every interaction, we are both **teacher** and **student**.

UNPACKING THE PROCESS OF THIS EXAMPLE

1. **Rung of the Spiral:** Classroom = Anxiety

2. **Experience:** Physical suffering, panic, fear, isolation, feeling lost, unsupported, alone

3. **Turning point:** Becoming open to what this classroom/ experience is about for us, which arrives in one's Divine timing

4. **Shift in consciousness:** Increased awareness arises around thoughts, beliefs

5. **Awareness which will birth the gifts:** Understanding the pattern of our thoughts and how they are contributing to the anxiety/awareness of beliefs that we don't feel safe in the world and are unsupported/awareness of sensitivity to other's energies and how that contributes to the anxiety

6. **Consciously creating anew:** Begin learning to redirect our thoughts and be in the present moment/begin to create new beliefs around safety and supportiveness

7. **Completion:** Birthing of a new level of self-esteem-changing beliefs around what we are capable of/and self-worth-value self enough to apply self-care and the supportive tools we've learned

8. **Summary - Gifts gained:** Awareness, acceptance, understanding, self-supportiveness/uplevelled self-esteem and self-worth/fostering deeper self-love

At this point of the completion of the classroom, we are now ready to graduate to the next level. If we were operating from perfectionism, we might not recognize we gained anything because, at this point, we may still be experiencing anxiety. From the perspective of completion, we have fulfilled the purpose of the initial classroom, which, while more intense, was intended to **initiate** awareness.

The next level may be where we learn to manage our energies, retrain our thoughts and rescript our beliefs. The next rung after this level may be where we no longer experience anxiety and are now gaining confidence to share our knowledge with others.

Sometimes it can appear as if we have regressed on the spiral, and it may feel like we're back in a previous classroom; however, it will be a different version this time. For example, you may experience a return of anxiety after a long period of its absence.

This next rendition is, in fact, a new rung on the spiral. Sometimes the Soul chooses to learn in stages, making it a more leisurely ride, especially for the personality. There is also a period needed after our experience to integrate and assimilate what we have just learned and gained. If we find ourselves in a similar experience, it means we are going deeper with it, and there's more still to learn. This process gets easier as we begin to understand the steps of it, and with less resistance, we can often move through the experience with more trust, grace, and awareness.

As we rise in consciousness, we don't need the same types of classrooms, and we start to experience more joy, peace, and freedom. Ultimately, the point of the process is to awaken to the illusions of the beliefs we carry that keep us disconnected and limited in fear. We are rebirthed each time we rise to the next level, and a new version of ourselves wants to come through. Essentially, the path is a continuous cycle of birth, death, rising, and rebirth. The death stage is the shedding of the previous versions we've been holding within ourselves and releasing any beliefs and perceptions that no longer serve us. **The alchemy of the uplevelling process is releasing who we no longer want to be, remembering our true essence of love, and creating the new version we want to be and express in the world!**

SACRED CHOICE

What and who we choose to give our precious energy to is ours and ours alone!

When we have the **courage** to choose to face our doubts and fears, we allow our inner strength to bubble up. When we remain curious, we are open to seeing and receiving new opportunities and possibilities. When we allow ourselves to be **Teachable**, we release resistance and pretentiousness. **When we choose to go within, we open to the wisdom of the Universe, which will whisper and reveal understandings otherwise not comprehendible.**

This is the grace from which we can create! Are we ready to believe in ourselves? Are we willing to accept our worthiness? This is our path of reclaiming our Freedom! This is our Soul Calling!

Are we ready to choose?

AFFIRMATIONS

I am the Power and Presence of the Divine.

My path is illuminated before me.

I am worthy! I am enough!

MEDITATION ~ 'I INTEND SELF-WORTH'

Sit in a comfortable position. Straighten the spine. Gently roll the shoulders back and down, opening the heart space. Close the eyes, bringing focus to the Third Eye, the point between the eyebrows.

Place the base of your palms together, tips of the little fingertips touching, tips of the thumb tips touching. The rest of the fingers are extended up and the palms are open like they are a blooming flower. (If this is uncomfortable place palms together in prayer position.)

Begin to connect and deepen the breath. Slowly inhaling through the nostrils, allowing life to enter in. Slowly exhale from the mouth, releasing any heaviness, tension, or fear.

Tune into your heart space by bringing your awareness to your heart chakra. Tune into the beating of your heart. Then tune into the energy in your lower belly. Feel the energy flow up your spine on your inhale. Feel the energy flow down your spine on your exhale. Do this for a few breaths.

Set an intention to remember who you are, or silently ask, *'Who Am I?'*

Begin to inhale through the nose, exhale and softly chant 'SHHHHHHH' *(Continue this for 7 mins)*

To close, bring your hands back into prayer position, palms together at your heart space. Tune into how you feel—simply allowing.

Affirm that you are an essence of the Divine Presence. Affirm you are Love. Affirm you are worthy to be here. Affirm you have tremendous value because you are a sacred being (flaws and all).

Set your intention for the remainder of your day or evening.

We are One. We are Light. We are Love. We are Free.
(Total 11 minutes. Feel free to shorten or lengthen)

INSIGHTS & JOURNALING ~ *Freedom 1,2,3*

In your own journal or on the pages to follow in this book, take some time to ponder your answers to the following questions.

1. *"Our energy decreases when we give our attention to anything outside us that creates a drain, imbalance, or inequality."*
   - Where might you be losing your power and energy?
   - Make a list of all things that create a drain, imbalance, or inequality in your life.
   - Spend time pondering how your life could change if you could reinstate your balance and energy in each scenario.

2. *"We are what we believe ourselves to believe." Paulo Coelho.*
   - What do you believe about yourself, your attributes, and your capabilities?
   - Where do you hold harsh judgments on yourself?
   - What beliefs are you carrying that might be keeping you from living a more Soul-infused life?

3. *"When we release our attachments to what others think, we cultivate freedom and harmony, and we can "live and let live."*
   - How comfortable are you with following your heart when others cannot or will not understand or accept your choices?
   - How often do you choose your inner resonance and Soul whispers when the outside world and the people closest to you are not in agreement?
   - What do you feel in your body as you contemplate your answers to these questions?
   - Do you feel alignment, authenticity, and resonance or do you feel a tightening in your chest or elsewhere in your body?

Chapter 5:

Exploring Soul Language: Connecting to Resonance

"What lies behind us and what lies before us are small matters compared to what lies within us."

Ralph Waldo Emerson

SOUL INFUSED PERSONALITY

Alignment to our spiritual strength and highest path to freedom is the journey inward, to our hearts. Understanding and knowing ourselves arrive from going within, as our heart is the gateway to connecting and cultivating a deep connection with our Soul, our Higher Self.

The more we align and call forth our Soul, the stronger the infusion becomes, fostering a deep trust with our Soul that then nurtures, develops, and brings forth a Soul-infused personality. Once we've become more Soul-infused, we continue to expand further and are more and more energized with our Soul's essence.

INCARNATIONAL BLUEPRINT

When the Soul is designing the blueprint for the upcoming incarnation, there is tremendous care and consideration to what the themes will be. Because the Soul is on a continuum, there will be a review of previous lives and a selection of what experiences and themes need to continue. The Soul then decides what it hopes to learn, master, and complete for the upcoming life. There is also a consideration as to which gifts, talents, and abilities will be brought forth.

The blueprint is like a roadmap and consists of fated connections and experiences, potential destiny, and ultimate expression! This earth school is one of free will, which is why there will be potential and not absolute experiences.

For instance, say a Soul has been working on mastering the Soul quality forgiveness. On the continuum, the Soul will choose lives and experiences of being both perpetrator and victim, for there cannot be a complete understanding of forgiveness if one hasn't both experienced being forgiven and having to forgive!

In this example, imagine the Soul has experienced **having to forgive through** many lives, and the lesson hasn't yet been completed to the degree of completion or mastery the Soul has intended. Therefore forgiveness, particularly **to forgive,** is intended in the blueprint. The Soul then calls in another Soul who would agree to play the role of one who will play out an experience that will provide an opportunity for forgiveness. *(Maybe it's a spouse who betrays through infidelity.)*

The invited Soul agreeing to play this role will do so as long as it's congruent with their Soul's plan or offers learning, growing, and healing for the Soul. It's always a complementary dynamic of our programming, healing, and growth. There is a sophisticated and multidimensional choreography between our lives and interactions.

In this example, the Soul playing the spouse would be considered a **fated** connection, and yet, because of free will, this Soul will also have to grow or achieve certain things pertaining to their blueprint before this meeting can occur. Therefore, other Souls will agree to come forth if, for some reason, the circumstance of this intended connection isn't viable.

Free will is always a variable; therefore, the blueprint is created with this in mind, which is why the Soul sets the blueprint up with potentials rather than absolutes. The intention is to learn or master something, and the 'how' that happens or the classrooms that will provide the background opportunities aren't necessarily set in stone. It's like a constantly moving chess board.

In the blueprint, there will be an intention of mastery and lessons to be fulfilled, and there will also be paths of service. This is where we can contribute to applying our gifts and talents, where our deeper paths of fulfillment awaken.

This blueprint is truly a moving, dynamic map. We are always playing out, learning, and contributing through our gifts and talents. They are interconnected in intricate ways, along with the complexity of the synergy of the relationships and experiences we are engaged in!

The Soul won't force the personality; a big part of our transformation is learning to discern what the personality pursuits are compared to the Soul's vision and purpose.

The challenge in this is that the ego mind tends to narrate events and experiences because it wants to logically understand what is happening. This can create obstacles to us growing in the shortest path possible, with the least amount of resistance, because we get caught up more in the story and drama than the meaning and purpose of what's occurring (classroom).

Also, when dealing with the heart, some things aren't logical and cannot be comprehended with our intelligence, which is why it's so important to connect with our Soul and get to know our Soul's essence intimately.

DISCERNMENT AND RESONANCE

The more we call forth and feel the Soul's presence, love, peace, and strength, the clearer and more discerning we become on what the whispers of our Soul are compared to the projections of our personality.

The Soul speaks to us through resonance, which feels like an inner, harmonious alignment. This isn't to say the path of resonance is always the easiest one, yet there will be a sense of knowing it is our truth and for our highest good.

There can be a fine line between our discerning mind and fear. Ultimately, anything coming from Spirit and our Soul will never create or propagate fear. If we do feel a response of fear, then that could be the unresolved energy of fear arising to be processed. It could also be a notification that we are caught up in a story or thought form, and we can then choose to course correct and realign to a different frequency like optimism or faith.

It is most beautiful when we honor our inner resonance because it removes judgment. We simply seek whether something is in alignment with us in each moment, day and experience. We don't need to explore the why, and we can transcend the polarity of having to see something as good/bad or right/wrong. If it resonates with us, it's because our Soul is guiding us towards the fulfillment of our unique blueprint. We can come from an understanding that what may be true for us may not be so for another. From this place, we can lovingly and authentically **live and let live. We can be free and give freedom!**

Body Wisdom. Another way to discern what is our inner resonance is with a body check. Especially when experiencing a painful personal matter or if we're going through a stormy time, it can be more challenging to be clear. The Soul also communicates through the body, which is another way to hear our guidance.

Generally, when it's of resonance, the body will expand and feel lighter. When not, the body will contract, and we may hold our breath and feel a recoiling or a heaviness.

It can take practice to discover when the body responds from a place of not resonating versus fear. To clarify this difference, sit for a moment with your eyes closed. Take a few breaths, release any tension on the exhales, and tune into the heart. Now think of a place, person, pet, or time that has brought absolute love or joy. Notice the body's response and what and where feelings of expansion, warmth, or lightness are.

Then call to mind something that doesn't feel good or in alignment. Again, notice the body's response.

Non-Resonance vs. Fear. Think of something that creates fear, and pay attention to any contractions or sensations in the body. Now tune into something that resonates and feels aligned. Notice the changes in the body. Tune into any subtle differences between the two scenarios.

When it is fear, there may be more of a gut contraction or a chill. There will be a different, albeit subtle, response when there is non-resonance. It may feel like a deep knowing. The more we are open to discovering the contrasts, the more we learn to listen to our inner guidance system, which includes Soul and body guidance.

The more we practice this, the more we develop our **clear discerning muscle,** and we can, in an instant, be aware and confident when it's resonance or fear.

LANGUAGE OF THE SOUL

Presence of Soul. The Soul communicates in more of a whisper than a roar. **Soul Speak** is subtle, neutral, loving, and at times can even feel detached because it isn't entangled in the story. Soul will gently nudge yet never force. There is a specific essence signature to our Soul. Once we allow this presence and deepen our connection, this companionship becomes tangible and palpable, just like any other relationship.

This is relevant to mention because one of the challenges with connecting, and more importantly, **trusting our Soul**, occurs because the personality is accustomed and conditioned to put belief and faith into what it can see, hear, taste, and prove on the physical level.

The world can be loud, and the more outward we are focused, which is what the personality (ego self) is geared to, the harder it is to hear our Soul. This can create an illusionary separation from our rich inner world, our **authentic self.**

The result is a lack of trust in our inner guidance. Even though our Soul is always trying to shine through and communicates with us, if we aren't nurturing our Soul relationship, outer pulls or others' opinions will eclipse our Divine counsel.

The other effect is we may end up not trusting anything or anyone because we will be experiencing life and our classrooms purely from ego, which generates survival consciousness. This fosters more fear, judgment, separation, pain, suffering, and struggle, all of which strengthen the ego self.

We may then begin to feel like we must do it all on our own, that no one really cares and that we are alone, so we end up closing off physical and spiritual support, creating even more fragmentation, sorrow, and emptiness.

Another key for us to remember in this free will school is that we have so many beings yearning to assist us and can only do so upon our **asking and receiving.** We are never truly alone, and nothing is impossible in Spirit.

At some point, we are invited to ask ourselves if we are open to this guidance and willing to invoke their assistance. Are we ready to work as a collaborative team with the Divine Presence and all the spiritual helpers waiting for our invocation?

Art of Listening. Learning to hear our Soul's guidance can be a process in and of itself because this communication is often subtle, as the Soul operates at a pure and higher frequency. Our physical body is made of matter, which is denser, meaning it vibrates at a slower frequency. Emotions are less dense than the physical body yet more dense than thoughts. Each of these states is energy operating at different frequencies and reverberating into the field around us. This is the premise of cause and effect: what we project out has an equal and opposite reaction, so we will attract back to us that which we put out. For example, when we align to love, we are attracting love, as when we align to fear, we attract more fear.

While our thoughts and emotions are connected because emotions are a closer frequency to the physical density, what we feel is the most important element when consciously creating and manifesting.

Because of the premise of free will, the Universe and the subconscious are impartial. This design supports our freedom as conscious creators.

We cannot fool energy, meaning that just thinking positively doesn't always bring us what we intend. Ultimately our frequency determines what we generate and attract.

When we connect more deeply and consciously with our Soul, we organically uplift the frequency of our mind, body, and emotions and authentically raise our resonance.

Calm Waters. Imagine our mental, emotional and physical bodies combined as a body of water, such as a lake. The Soul is the sand at the bottom of the lake. When our mind is overactive, we are emotionally charged or physically tense; the lake waters become stormy and cloudy. The more intense this is, the more difficult it is to see the bottom of the lake. Similarly, the more turbulent we are mentally, emotionally, and physically, the more difficult it is to hear our guidance (to see the bottom of the lake).

This is why processing our emotions, calming our mind, and learning to release tension and move energy in our bodies is so important. Activities such as being in nature, meditating, journaling, creating, exercising, yoga, chi gong, or anything life-giving can bring joy, inspiration, and contentment and facilitate **our becoming calm waters.**

Redefining Surrender. Becoming calm waters requires trust, and because we have been operating from survival consciousness, we have deep programming not to trust. Even our nervous systems need to recalibrate to be more aligned with the parasympathetic state rather than the sympathetic *fight-or-flight* response.

The irony of being in survival is that it sets up programming to betray ourselves, our **authentic Soul self.** This is a deterrent because if we are in fear, we are being run by ego and will most likely not be clear on who or what we trust. Ultimately, we are learning to trust ourselves, our **Soul Self,** to the degree that we can have the courage to honor our blueprint and walk our path, our true north!

When we are Soul-infused, we have the courage to feel all our positive and negative emotions without attachment or judgment. We can be ourselves unapologetically and learn, unlearn, and relearn with an open mind, again and again. We can honor our inner truth, even if it's uncomfortable or unpopular.

To have the courage to be grounded in our hearts and to live with purpose and meaning, with the stamina to carry forth with grit, resiliency, awareness, care, and balance.

Our Soul may not communicate with a roar, yet Soul-infused, we become fiercely strong, passionate, and loving with the gentleness only the Soul can weave, like the lion/lioness essence!

As Brene Brown expressed, **strong back, soft front**. Our spine's become as strong as steel; our hearts are radiantly open, warm, and compassionate. This is our invitation, our path to freedom.

Grace Of Surrender. This isn't an easy concept or act for most of us. Partly because it may feel contradictory to our self-preservation and because surrender is often misunderstood. To soften and allow our Soul forth, we may need to redefine surrender because this is precisely what we need to do to become Soul-infused.

The ego's definition of surrender is to give up, abdicate, concede defeat, fail, abandon, cave in, and be a victim. It is a consciousness of hopelessness and helplessness.

The Soul defines surrender as aligning, connecting, unifying, bonding, devoting, softening, and connecting. It is a consciousness of courageous alignment to the flow of all life—a sacred allowing and merging, a coming **home**, and the foundation of **deep intimacy**.

Where our energy goes indicates our deeper (usually unconscious) underlying beliefs. Are we directing more towards love or fear? The

Soul's path is one of **love and connection, allowing our faith in love to be stronger than our faith in fear.**

We get to choose!!!

AFFIRMATIONS

I call forth my Soul.

I surrender to the grace and guidance of my Soul.

I choose Love.

MEDITATION ~ 'I INTEND FAITH'

This meditation can be done lying down or in a comfortable seated position. If seated, place the thumb tips to the index fingertips.

Close the eyes and begin to connect to the breath, inhaling slowly, exhaling slowly for a few cycles. Allow yourself to become present in your breath, body, and heart space. Gently noticing any areas in your body of heaviness, tension, or contraction and slowly begin to soften and intentionally send the breath to those spaces.

Call forth your Soul or expand into your Soul. Take a moment to feel the presence of your Soul's light, strength, lightness, and peace. (It's okay if you don't feel anything, your Soul is present, and you are receiving the vibrations by simply consciously connecting. If not a visualizer, set your intention or honor where you're guided).

Visualize an ocean, lake, or pond. And imagine there is a raging storm where the winds are whipping, the waves are gray and tumultuous. The sky is dark and fierce. Begin to breathe deeper, slowing down your exhale. Imagine with each exhale, the storm, wind, and waves are calming. There is a break in the clouds, and the light of the sun/moon begins to shine through.

The sky is now calm and clear. The water is pristinely still. So much so you can see or feel the bottom of the ocean, lake, or pond. Imagine a beautiful, luminescent light that begins to rise from the bottom. It's warm, loving, peaceful, and tranquil. You feel a sense of home.

Bask in this light. Knowing you are safe, loved, seen, and cared for. Feel that you matter to this presence. Just Be!

Slowly come back to your breath and body. Gently bringing movement to your fingers and toes, deepening your breath. Rub palms together, creating heat. Then place your palms over your eyes or ears. Feel the warmth. Gently affirm that you are present, back in your body, and in the present moment.

Set an intention to connect with your Soul often throughout your day.

We are One. We are Light. We are Love. We are Free.

(Total 11 minutes. Feel free to shorten or lengthen)

INSIGHTS & JOURNALING ~ *Freedom 1,2,3*

In your own journal or on the pages to follow in this book, take some time to ponder your answers to the following questions.

1. *"The more we align and call forth our Soul, the stronger the infusion becomes, fostering a deep trust with our Soul that then nurtures, develops, and brings forth a Soul-infused personality. Once we've become more Soul-infused, we continue to expand further and are more and more energized with our Soul's essence."*
   - What do you need to deepen your faith and trust?
   - Do you have any blocks or resistance?
   - Is there anything blocking your connection to your Soul, Spirit?

2. *"There can be a fine line between our discerning mind and fear. Ultimately, anything coming from Spirit and our Soul will never create or propagate fear."*
   - How clear are you when it comes to discerning between your inner resonance and personality-ego-based fear?
   - What guides you in your discernment? Where do you feel it? How do you know?

3. *"**Redefining Surrender.** Becoming calm waters requires trust, and because we have been operating from survival consciousness, we have deep programming not to trust."*
   - Where are you in the process of **surrender?**
   - Do you have any fear?
   - What do you feel in your body as you contemplate your answers to these questions?
   - Do you need to redefine surrender?

Chapter 6:

Liberating Our Minds: Realizing Our Potential

"Know your mind! Know it's Divine."

Jai Jagdeesh

UNDERSTANDING OUR MINDS

Our perception becomes our reality! Therefore, a significant element of becoming a Soul-infused personality, expressing the highest potential of our Divine blueprint, and claiming our sovereignty includes the training of our mind. Understanding our mind facilitates deeper awareness which fosters insight into the lens that filters our experiences. Once we have this recognition, we can begin learning to relate to everything differently if we choose.

The **Conscious Mind** is where we filter our experiences via our five senses. This is the seat of our identity as a personality, ego, and logical mind. It is also referred to as our concrete and the **Lower Mind**.

This mind filters experiences through discernment. If there hasn't yet been a strong unification with the Soul, the personality will most often perceive each encounter and event through the lens of fear. This then sets up for more experiences of separation, conflict, drama, and, of course, the continued attraction of fear.

The **Subconscious Mind,** our abstract mind, is connected to our Soul essence, our **Higher Self**. This mind is an instrument for the Soul and, when directed by our **sovereign self**, is known as the **Higher Mind.** Unresolved energies, programming, beliefs, and records of our experiences flow through this mind. This mind never sleeps and is always aware and vigilant.

The **Superconscious Mind** is the universal mind, also called the quantum field.

The universal mind illuminates the Soul, which then radiates the conscious mind. When this unification and alignment occurs, the universal mind functions as a guide to the conscious mind as it can weave elements of life into more beautiful patterns and new possibilities. **It is infinite creativity and intelligence.**

What's possible? When our intelligence is connected with our heart and the universal mind, we become a clear channel to serve the Divine Mind and are liberated from the bonds of matter. The mind fulfills its purpose of being a channel for the pure flow of Higher Mind energy allowing the personality to become a clear channel. We can then express Divine Love and fulfill our Divine Purpose in a high and refined manner.

FURTHER EXPLORATION OF THE SUBCONSCIOUS MIND

The subconscious mind plays a pivotal role in how we behave, react, vibrate and experience life; therefore it's instrumental to understand it a little deeper.

A visual of its complexity is to imagine a sea surrounded by a beautiful, dynamic landscape that influences the sea like the weather and moon affect our oceans. Imagine there are also several rivers and streams flowing into the sea. Some of these rivers are programming that includes inherited, collective, and personal Soul programming.

Other rivers are unresolved energies, traumas, and experiences from our past lives. These come from the Akashic records, which are like our own library containing the memory of every thought, feeling, deed, word, and experience our Soul has ever had.

When the Soul has an experience, it's ultimately choosing to do so for its higher purpose, learning, growing, or healing. The personality must be able to process the energies of that experience, and if that doesn't happen in that incarnation, then the unresolved energies get uploaded into the Akashic records. Because of the nature of energy, what hasn't been balanced, harmonized, transformed, or transmuted will show up in a future incarnation to be resolved.

When a Soul reincarnates, the Soul's blueprint for that specific incarnation determines what gets activated and downloaded. As the Soul evolves and raises consciousness, more activations and downloading from the akashic records will ensue. Soul programs are the classrooms we've chosen to experience here in earth school. Additional rivers and streams come from the current incarnation, including inner child aspects, incarnational events, dramas, and traumas.

This all flows through the subconscious mind.

This mind also acts as a filter, meaning it takes in all we hear and see. It doesn't differentiate between reality and fantasy, so when we are watching a movie, the news, or playing a video game, it's as if it is happening in the present time to the body and psyche. So, if we are playing a war game, those energies are picked up in our energy field and processed through our physiology and aura like we are engaged in a real-life battle.

This is important because from a frequency standpoint, what we surround ourselves with becomes a part of our vibration as energy is also transferrable, which is why it is said that we are equally responsible for the energy we put out and the energy we allow in. If we intend and learn to activate our Conscious Creator, then we are also apprentices of understanding the different octaves of energy frequencies.

Because lower frequencies are denser, there is more of a gravitational pull with them. It can be a process to train oneself to hold higher frequencies.

Imagine we are in a light and positive mood and meet up with a group of friends. Suppose the conversation becomes gossipy and unkind about a particular person. Because this is a lower vibration of separatism, there will be an energetic heaviness associated with the discussion. We may find ourselves caught up in and participating without even realizing it until afterward. The fallout is that we are now aligned to weighted thoughts and emotions such as anger or frustration, depending on the nature of the dialogue and what triggered us from being drawn into the chat, such as guilt. There's a high probability we also lost our light and positive mood we had prior to the interaction.

This is often a part of our process that facilitates us becoming more aware. The next time we find ourselves in a similar situation, we may still get pulled into it. However, we may have a more conscious awareness that it is happening. And the time after that, we may be able not to participate at all and choose to hold a space of love or harmony instead. Or we may feel we need to remove ourselves from the situation altogether.

The more we know ourselves and are unified with our Soul, the quicker we will respond through our inner resonance. Remembering that the Soul cares for all life and beings, we will be guided to be aligned with higher frequencies of *thrive consciousness* and will be life-giving, all the while doing so without judgment. The more Soul-aligned we are, the more uncomfortable it becomes to hold and engage lower frequencies.

While we may get to a point where we are predominantly in a vibration of love or peace, we will still have programming and unresolved energies rising, whether coming up from the subconscious for resolution or because the Soul is seeking an experience.

The difference is that we will now understand what is playing out, and we can allow the energies to flow through and be processed. We will be mindful that we are in a classroom that ultimately serves our growth and can seek out the more profound meaning and purpose of what we are experiencing. We will have the clarity and means to apply our **supportive tools*** to help us navigate.

We have included Supportive Tools in our Resources Section at the end of the book.

Grounded in our Soul power, we will have the grace and grit to choose our alignment, and responses and shift perceptions of what is happening, keeping us within our power. We can have the mental mastery to simultaneously be present with what is and be more precise and intentional on what we want to create and experience next without attachment or expectation.

We are free to be in the flow of life, allowing what is to be, honoring the sacredness of the moment, and trusting that what is unfolding will birth transformation. The less resistance there is, the smoother and quicker we move through the experience. This also opens the opportunity to learn more through awareness, so even though we will still have some experiences, they become less intense. We can evolve quicker without having the same type of classrooms we previously needed for growth and healing. In essence, our classrooms change.

Dreams are also processed through the subconscious. Sometimes our Soul, spiritual helpers, and loved ones who have transitioned communicate with us and send us messages through our dreams. Often, however, our dreams are a way of purging out the subconscious, so what we haven't been able to process in waking time gets processed this way. Like watching a movie or playing a video game, we experience what we dream of as if it's actually happening. This is why we may wake from our dreams feeling the emotional remnants of it or being physically tired and sore.

The subconscious is like an obedient servant, responding directly to what it's hearing. For example, if we have an event coming up and we repeat to ourselves that we don't want to be sick for the event, the subconscious hears sick, not that we don't want to be sick. When we phrase it as we want to be healthy, it hears health and responds accordingly. This is because it operates on frequency. When we think or say sick, it holds a different frequency than healthy. That's the power of the word. When we relate to the subconscious in this manner, knowing it is always listening, we learn to be much more mindful and precise about what we think and intend.

When we find ourselves behaving, reacting, or out bursting in shocking ways or manners beyond our conscious intent, this is our subconscious purging. When energy builds and rises to a point it needs to release, it will override our conscious mind. Therefore, just wanting or intending to manifest rarely works in the long run. In this new paradigm, working with our subconscious and frequency is imperative. Without a shift in consciousness, we won't be able to sustain the higher frequency or the manifested desire.

For example, if we want more ease yet we have unresolved energies of struggle or beliefs that we must work hard to attain what we wish for (*subconscious*), then we will continue to experience struggle rather than ease. When we become aware of these energies and beliefs, we can process them (transform or transmute) and create new beliefs.

Remembering that subconscious is like an obedient servant, we can retrain and reinstruct it with new frequencies and beliefs.

A powerful exercise is to explore beliefs we hold on ourselves, life, money, sexuality, humanity, men, women, gender, our past, etc. While some beliefs will be quickly identifiable, others can be challenging to root because they are sown deeply into the fabric of our subconscious. We may have carried them over from past lives or have been so deeply conditioned that we don't even recognize it is there.

We often need to identify a pattern to discover the underlying belief that is running. For example, someone suggests we believe it is unsafe to be in an intimate relationship. We may respond and feel that we don't think that is true. When we look back at the patterns in our relationships, we may become aware that there's been a predominant theme of being abused, manipulated, or taken advantage of in some way that has caused significant pain and trauma.

This could present a bit differently in each relationship and with different people, yet there will be a common thread, theme, or essence of the belief. When a pattern is running, maintaining it is an underlying belief.

Using this example, the belief could also be that people are abusive or that we don't deserve love and kindness. It could be different for each of us, so when we explore this, we want to keep investigating it until we feel we have identified the core belief.

Belief Systems

I am ~~not good enough~~.	I am (good) enough.
I have to ~~work hard to be successful~~.	I align to success with ease and flow.
~~Life is hard~~.	Life is easy and gentle.
I will be ~~hurt if I open my heart~~.	It is safe for me to open my heart.

To create a new belief system, draw a line down the middle of a page. Write the old belief on the left side, cross it out, and then replace it by creating a new one.

For example, I believe it is unsafe for me to be in an intimate relationship (cross it out) and replace it with, I am safe and supported in all of my relationships.

Sometimes the awareness of a belief is enough to transmute it. For stickier ones, we may want to use our new belief as an affirmation, repeating it often throughout the day. It is also powerful to write out or say out loud that we **now declare, instruct and intend our subconscious to believe on every level that it is safe for me...** *(insert new belief/affirmation).*

It's important we practice feeling it and holding that frequency for a minimum of 20 seconds. Using this example, we could think of a place or time we felt safe and then hold that feeling of safety. If feeling it isn't attainable (*not everyone is a 'feeler'*), try to visualize or hear it. It can be customized for what works for us individually.

We can tune into the frequency and repeat the affirmation simultaneously, or they can be alternated. Keeping it simple for ourselves will create a solid foundation for sustainable change. It's about finding what works for us and keeping it as light and manageable as possible.

Periodically exploring our beliefs is beneficial because as we heal and shift consciousness, we may uncover or have access to an awareness we previously were not ready for or didn't have.

This process guides and teaches us to become more aware of limiting beliefs, perceptions, attitudes, illusions, and delusions we hold. We learn how to choose to release thoughts and beliefs that are no longer serving us and making us feel like a victim, bringing us to freedom of mind and being and to the remembrance that we are powerful, sovereign Souls!

It's important to remember to stay out of comparison and judgment with self and others, be as gentle, loving, and nurturing as possible, and keep returning to this when we get off course or out of our center. Which we will. There will always be an ebb and flow in our lives and processes.

OUR JOURNEY IS RELATIVE

Each one of us will have our unique journey.

The complexity of our incarnational journey is such that we could be healing intense and painful trauma from past lives, yet our lives to the outer could appear easy and blessed. This understanding is essential because if it is our experience, we may feel guilty for some of the feelings we have and are processing. Or we may deny them because we may feel we need only to focus on the goodness of our lives, and we shouldn't feel like we do because our lives are filled with blessings.

85

Others of us may have experienced significant trauma in this current incarnation and healing past lives. ***It is said from certain spiritual concepts that over 90% of what we experience in everyday life originated from past lives.***

When there has been current incarnational trauma, the path of healing can be a bit more complex and different. Most traumas occur as chosen classrooms for a Soul's healing or growth. While there will always be value for the individual Soul experiencing this, there can also be additional reasons the Soul has chosen the trauma experiences, such as to facilitate evolution or healing for the Soul family, lineage (which includes birth family), a culture, a country, or as part of facilitating evolution for the human species and or Mama Earth as just some examples.

There is a misconception that if something terrible happens, it's because it is a payback based on past actions. While this is sometimes the Soul's way of balancing energies, the Soul may also choose to have trauma or drama for the actual experience of it, to play a different role. The choreography of our lives is more multi-dimensional than linear.

The point is that things aren't always as they seem. The more we are open to this, the more patient, understanding, and loving we can be. For ourselves, others, and all beings. All life! It's genuinely so much bigger than us. Yet we are intricately as worthy and honored as every Soul and being because we all contain the nectar of Divine intelligence. We are learning to understand that we are an insignificant grain of sand and as important as the brightest sun. From a life-thriving consciousness, we cannot be separate, better or worse than any other living being or essence that contains this nectar.

The leaf doesn't look at other leaves or the branch of the tree and reflect disdain, inferiority, or superiority. It understands the flow, synergy, and purpose of both itself as an individualized leaf and that of the branch, and of the whole tree. That it is as important and purposeful as the branch. Different expressions, yet not separate. All part of the whole. Individuated yet connected. It can even understand the importance and necessity of the wind that blows it, the insects that invade it, and the sun and rain that nurture and provide what is needed for its growth and continued prolific evolution. And it allows, when time, the release of its form as a leaf, releasing from the branch, falling to the ground, and re-emerging to Mama Earth to be transmuted and transformed.

AFFIRMATIONS

I intend to unify my mind with the Divine mind.

I am beautiful, unique, and blessed.

I am a Divine diamond.

MEDITATION ~ 'I INTEND CONSCIOUS AWARENESS'

Sit in a comfortable seated position. Straighten the spine. Gently roll the shoulders back and down, opening the heart space. Close the eyes, bringing focus to the Third Eye, the point between the eyebrows. Palms are open and upward, relaxing the back of your wrists on the top of your knees or thighs.

Begin to bring gentle awareness to the body, noticing any place you're holding tension or tightness. Begin to soften those spaces, relaxing the shoulders down a bit more. Slowly inhale from the nostrils, exhale from the mouth. Do this 3x.

Imagine a vast ocean—beautiful, deep, mysterious. Intend to gently release, from 'your ocean', anything that is no longer serving your highest good. That what you are ready to see, know and understand is lovingly brought to your awareness.

Begin to inhale slowly through the nose, exhale softly and slowly chanting 'Hummmmm'.

As you begin to chant 'Hummmmm', press the thumb tip to index fingertip, then thumb tip to middle fingertip, then thumb tip to ring fingertip, then thumb tip to little fingertip. Inhale palms open, exhale and repeat chanting 'Hummmmm' while pressing the fingertips. Continue this cycle. (Continue for 7 mins)

 (Beginning of the chant starts with the thumb tip to the index fingertip. Try and space the time you're holding each fingertip equally. By the time you're finished your 'Hummmmm' chant, you are ending at the thumb tip and little finger)

Sit quietly, allowing the energy to flow. Notice how you feel, how your body feels. Tune into the center of your being—the expansiveness of your energy field.

Rub your palms together, creating heat, then place your palms anywhere on your body you feel needs some extra attention, touch, or healing. Then place your palms together at the heart center in prayer position. Taking a deep breath in through the nose, exhale slowly through the mouth. Set your intention for the remainder of your day or evening.

We are One. We are Light. We are Love. We are Free.

(Total 11 minutes. Feel free to shorten or lengthen)

INSIGHTS & JOURNALING ~ *Freedom 1,2,3*

In your own journal or on the pages to follow in this book, take some time to ponder your answers to the following questions.

1. *"This mind [the subconscious mind] also acts as a filter, meaning it takes in all we hear and see. It doesn't differentiate between reality and fantasy, so when we are watching a movie, the news, or playing a video game, it's as if it is happening in the present time to the body and psyche."*

   - Being aware of the subconscious mind as a filter, explore the physical, mental and emotional effects of some of the choices you are making. What do you need to deepen your faith and trust?
   - How do you feel after watching certain movies or how do feel when you speak to yourself?
   - Where do you want to see less energy or more energy?

2. *"Because lower frequencies are denser, there is more of a gravitational pull with them. It can be a process to train oneself to hold higher frequencies."*
   - What frequencies would you like to align with more?
   - What support do you need to become more steadily aligned?

3. *"Periodically exploring our beliefs is beneficial because as we heal and shift consciousness, we may uncover or have access to an awareness we previously were not ready for or didn't have."*
   - Explore your beliefs around different categories such as yourself, your life, your passions, love, freedom, humanity money, and more.
   - What beliefs need to be released?
   - For each one that you choose to release, write a new one to replace the old one.

Chapter 7:

Mastering the Mind

"No one has ever been able to control their thinking, although people may tell the story of how they have. I don't let go of any of my thoughts; I meet them with understanding. They let go of me."

Byron Katie

On average, we have about 1000 thoughts per second. Out of these, the ones we predominantly attach to and begin running in our minds are the ones that match the resonance of our beliefs, conditioning, fears, unresolved energies, or programming. These can come from the subconscious mind, the collective consciousness, thought forms, and world energies, as some examples.

Game Changer. Understanding this is a beginning step in our process of retraining our minds. This awareness allows an opportunity to create space between the thoughts and the thinker, confirming that we are not our thoughts. As we begin to comprehend this, awareness expands, and we start opening up to seeing our thought patterns, which are predominately the foundation of our narratives. Some examples include recognizing every time we go into the script of *I'm not good enough; I'm never acknowledged; nothing ever works out for me; I'm not respected; the world isn't safe; I have to struggle to succeed,* and more.

This realization facilitates change because we now have the cognizance to begin disrupting these patterns if we so choose.

Furthermore, when we know our mind and story, we are less likely to be caught up in others' mind webs. This supports us in honoring our inner resonance and standing firm in our sovereignty.

MIND IN TRAINING

Conditions of the Human Mind. Each moment offers a story of suffering or peace, and we *get to* choose which narrative we want. It sounds simple, yet there is so much suffering and conflict within ourselves, amongst each other, and on the planet.

Why is this, and most importantly, how can we change this? We generally filter our experiences and life through the discerning mind, our warning mind, which notifies us of potential danger. The pitfall is that we may come from fear rather than curiosity or trust. Some may approach life through more of a positive, optimistic mind filter and see the possibilities and potential in a situation, person, or relationship. When not balanced, the pitfall with this lens is that there can be a rose-colored glasses view. This can create blind spots where there isn't any discernment of potentially harmful consequences, and we may over-ride or not hear our inner resonance.

A **mind in training** is learning to **see from all perspectives.** This is called the meditative or neutral mind. The discerning and optimistic minds operate from more of a limited, dualistic approach where either may see something as wrong or good. At the same time, the neutral mind transcends the duality as it's not operating from a black or white outlook.

Imagine we see an accident at a corner in the road where there are also five other witnesses. Each of us is at different points in this corner, so we all have a different viewpoint of what happened, all of which may be accurate yet varied. Each view is incomplete in that it hasn't seen the event from all perspectives, the other points of the corner.

Imagine we are hovering above the scene and can see the whole picture. We can take in the details yet also see the bigger picture, which encompasses all the different views beholding more of a complete vision. The neutral mind is the observer; while it can take everything in, it takes nothing personally. This doesn't mean we are all void of emotion. From this perspective, we can feel and hold higher frequencies such as compassion, peace, and freedom because we are transcending the polarity.

Meditative Mind... Neutral Mind... Complete Mind. We cultivate this complete mind by learning to pause, observe, breathe, and *respond*. Once out of dichotomy, we can become responsive rather than reactive because we've created space to choose rather than rebound from the unconscious, wounded part of us. Essentially our process is coming out of the unconscious to the conscious.

Discerning Mind (Warning)	Neutral Mind	Optimistic Mind
Over-fearful	Can see from all perspectives	Over exuberant
Over-focused on consequences	Knowing	Can't see blind spots
Not trusting	Objective & non-reactive	Can be too trusting
Pessimistic	Transcends duality	Sees possiblities without consequences
↓ ⟶	**Balanced**	⟵ ↓
Dualism Limits Us		Dualism Limits Us

Lower Mind Meets Higher Mind. The lower mind, the egoic element of us conditioned to survive, generally operates from separatism, confusion, doubt, uncertainty, anger, boredom, and not feeling good enough.

Because fear is the underlying matrix fueling the lower mind, we operate more from restriction and protection rather than expansion and trust. We also filter through the lens of our life experiences, personality, and conditioning. Usually, this is based on *lack consciousness*, and therefore it isn't easy to see what's available to us. The egoic mind cannot see beyond what it has experienced. This is why it often operates either in the past or projecting fear of the future, creating anxiety. This happens because the egoic mind doesn't want to repeat the pain, loss, or suffering previously experienced.

Here lies the great contradiction of fear. We fear loss and suffering, and this generates more of the same. This is the insidious loop of the unconscious mind. Furthermore, because we are programmed to *survive*, we are primed to experience suffering and conflict. We become accustomed to this way of being, which creates unconscious desire and addiction to drama and suffering; it is often how we learn to feel *alive.*

When we are accustomed to conflict and drama, it takes time to re-acclimatize to the absence of this energy. Lower frequencies are heavier, and our bodies are denser, so we feel a rush of adrenaline from a fright, conflict, or dramatic situation in our body more than we do from a peaceful or serene experience.

An example of this is to imagine being in a plane ready for take-off. As the plane starts to rev up and accelerate on the runway, we can viscerally feel the vibration and energy of the speed and force. Once up in the air, when the plane levels out, a very calm space is entered, and it may take a moment to acclimate to the different vibrations. It can feel like nothing is happening and even feel like a letdown if we have been charged and adrenalized by the physical sensations. Upon leveling off, there can even be a sense of nothingness. Interestingly, we are now in less density and moving faster than on take-off. This is analogous to the process we may need to attune to when we start working with holding higher frequencies like love, peace, freedom, trust, compassion, etc.

Coming out of drama and conflict at first can feel like we are missing something, and we can even experience restlessness, boredom, and a sense of being in a void and untethered. In some instances, it can even present as strong withdrawal symptoms, like releasing an addiction. Therefore, learning to hold and align to higher vibrations and thoughts can be a process and training in and of itself.

Imagine we are trained to sing powerfully with the middle key of **C**. This is further strengthened because we sing with a large group in this same key. Now imagine we are training ourselves to sing 2 or 3 octaves above middle **C**. Training our vocal cords and getting comfortable singing something differently may take some time. Now imagine we have to learn to hold this higher octave note while we are in a group setting where they are still singing at the middle C note. This may also take additional training to learn to harmonize or still be able to hold our notes at a higher octave, both when we are alone in a quieter setting and a group setting. This is what it's like to begin training to hold higher frequencies. To do this, we need to become aware of our thoughts and the direction of our patterns. Otherwise, we will be hi-jacked by the group or collective energies more quickly, if not always.

To change our story, we need first to be aware of our story. When we begin to be mindful and take note of the patterns of our thoughts, we are revealed our narrative. There is a connection between our thoughts and our vibration. It is only when we begin to notice our thoughts and the frequency or energy signature associated with the thoughts we are thinking that we can start to adjust them.

When we change our thoughts, we shift our vibration. They are intricately connected. First comes the feeling, then the thought follows. The thoughts trigger more feelings which produce additional thoughts.

We are learning to be aware of this interaction and to balance this dance. So that our intending minds and magnetic emotions begin to work together to expand consciousness rather than fuel the unconscious programming of victim, martyr, suffering, separation, fear, and more.

Well-trodden pathways. When we continuously think the same themed thoughts, they become patterns. Which then become our narrative, our story. And therefore, our experiential reality. These thought patterns become like pathways. The more energy and attention given, the more well-trodden or entrenched they are. A trained mind has learned or is learning through *continuous refinement* to consciously create. It focuses on what is working, what is expanding, and where we have *arrived* vs. what is not going well or where we want to be.

We want to identify where our minds are holding us hostage and limiting us. Are our thoughts creating more restriction, criticism, and fear, or are they life-giving and expansive? Do they reflect the love in our hearts?

When we imagine our mind is like a garden and our thoughts are either weeds or flowers, we can approach this retraining in a more cultivating, nurturing, and gentle way. Knowing we will inevitably have weeds, we can seek them out neutrally and with the intention and purpose of creating the garden of our choosing.

This awareness will also reveal how we generally approach or relate to life, relationships, and ourselves. The 'glass half full or half empty' analogy reflects this because what we perceive, we experience. When we shift our viewpoint, the outer circumstance may not change, yet our experience of it ultimately does. **This is the power of our perception.**

Learning to implement a **perspective check** can be invaluable. This is when we pause, asking ourselves how we view, see, and relate to what we are thinking or experiencing.

For example, do we…

- Catastrophize
- Go into defeatism, deflation, abdication
- Respond with frustration, doubt, worry, anger, fear, etc. *(often or always)*

This awareness in and of itself is a disrupter and reveals our relationship with what we are experiencing in any given moment.

Outer Focus to Inner Focus. From a *survive consciousness*, we were predominantly seasoned to attune ourselves to the outer world rather than our inner one. This was necessary for previous paradigms as this could be the difference between us maintaining our livelihood or perishing. This was the foundation of self-preservation. Therefore as we move into *thrive consciousness*, we cultivate new thought patterns and pathways to explore and nurture our interior landscape. This is a significant shift in energy direction.

An example of how this may play out in our daily lives is when we have a trigger, like anger, from something someone said. Our initial reaction will often focus on the person and what was said, which fuels the anger even more. When we pause and check in with ourselves, identify the energy signature (*anger*), and disengage from the cause to focus on what's happening within us, we are now in a position to transmute or transform the anger energy. Additionally, we are creating a new response pathway, so it becomes easier and easier to *inner reply vs. outer reply*. We are also maintaining empowerment, and *inner authority,* because we aren't leaking or draining our energy by focusing on the outer.

This does not mean we accept abuse or bypass it to maintain peace because we don't like or want conflict; that would be *co-dependent consciousness*.

By focusing on our inner response and processing any related energy, we open up space for uplevelled frequencies, such as strength, peace, love, and more, and we can then respond vs. react from anger. If we respond from anger and with anger, we create more anger and react rather than respond.

Creating space by going inward, acknowledging and honoring what has been ignited within, we can now consciously reply rather than unconsciously backlash. This may also diffuse a conflict situation authentically, rather than co-dependently, because when we shift our focus off the outer environment and turn inward, there is an automatic vibrational shift in the dynamic. Energetically, for a dynamic to maintain itself, there has to be a reciprocity of energy, so when we pull out of that *current,* the energy, by its nature, creates a shift.

Thoughtforms. When we think of a thought repetitively enough, we create a thoughtform, which is similar to a cloud over our head. This cloud can be beautifully filled with inspiring elements or darker ones of fear and doom. It depends on the source of its creation.

When given enough energy, a thoughtform takes a life of its own.
It can only exist if we are still fueling it with our thoughts, yet at a
certain point, it literally becomes *a consciousness* and can, in turn,
begin to influence us. So when we fuel it, it fuels us, and we are in a
loop, usually very unconsciously.

Thoughtforms are one of the stages of manifestation as they contain
the potential to bring energy into form.

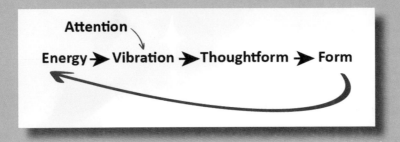

The intensity and duration that a thoughtform is nurtured is the
determining factor as to whether it actually comes into form. It's a
potential, and when we shift consciousness around the source of the
thoughtform, it can dissipate and, in some cases, instantly. When we
no longer give attention to the thoughts feeding the thoughtforms,
they can no longer influence us, which is great news if we've been
feeding them with weeds. Additionally, we can cultivate desired
thoughtforms bringing added value to our life by choosing to give
more energy to the thoughtforms we wish to cultivate into form.

Collective Thoughtforms, Collective Consciousness & Groupthink.
There are also **Collective Thoughtforms**, which can be very
influential because many people are contributing to them. This can
be in our favor in remarkable ways, such as when we tune into the
frequency of love. We are tuning into the thoughtform of love and

are being supported and uplifted by the energies of everyone aligned to this energy form.

Similarly, if we begin to fear something and continue to give our thoughts to a particular theme of fear, we become aligned to that fear's collective thoughtform. Say we start hearing of many people who have been diagnosed with breast cancer or people losing their jobs, and we start noticing we are having more and more thoughts of getting it, having it, or fearing we will experience that. If given enough energy, we will connect to the *collective thoughtform of breast cancer* or those who have *lost or fear losing their job*, which can exacerbate our fear.

Upon first understanding this, our trigger response may be to go into a fear that we are creating and manifesting what we fear. Or we will judge ourselves for being in fear. If this is the case, the most important thing to remind ourselves of is that the minute we are aware of this; we are disrupting the cording, the influence. If there is a shift in consciousness at that moment of awareness, it can be enough to unplug from the thoughtform. Other times we may need to redirect our thoughts elsewhere, detaching us from the thoughtform over time.

As we become more mindful of where our thoughts and energies are being directed, we can choose differently. And doing so, we are activating our **Conscious Creator Mind**.

The **Collective Consciousness** contains the energies, overflow, or unresolved energies of the species. An example of how this can impact us is imagining we have a global pandemic. This creates predominate fear in the species as a whole and, in turn, increases the overall intensity of fear on the planet, like a tsunami wave in the ocean.

Whether or not we are aware of the current of the collective consciousness, we can be significantly impacted or affected.

Groupthink is generally the mindset of the group we are around or in. This can range from a group of a few friends to a group with thousands or even millions. This includes a cultural, political, religious, or the *flavor of the month mindset*.

Interestingly, varying groups can bring out different *versions* of ourselves depending on the consciousness that shapes that particular crowd. Our programming, unresolved wounds, and desires determine our susceptibility to how or when we are more persuaded.

As everything is energy, when we are dealing with the **Collective Conscious** or **Groupthink**, we are dealing with energy *currents*. Like the strength of a river current, we can be swept up despite our best intentions: the larger the group, the more potential impact, and influence.

This is why we must learn to bring our focus inward and seek to authentically know ourselves and our **own true, unique north; our own current!**

The more we understand and accept all our *aspects, wounds, whys, gifts, and unique Divine blueprint,* the more grit we can access. Our roots anchor and go deep, and we are no longer susceptible to being fooled, misused, manipulated, or coerced.

When we come to know our mind is Divine, we no longer accept subjugation or oppression. From this consciousness, we understand our sovereignty and stand firm, hearts open and lights blazing!

From this place, we have the spiritual strength to honor our path, rise above tyranny, love the perceived unlovable, forgive the perceived unforgivable, and create the change that is perceived unchangeable.

To arrive here, we first must apply all of this to ourselves. To accept and embrace our own fractured, fragmented shadow elements. The path of wholeness is one of integration and unity. We have been trained and conditioned to believe we are inherently broken, flawed, or damaged. And is it from this consciousness of deceit that keeps us in bondage? From this, the mind becomes our fiercest persecutor and toughest opponent, our greatest limiter. With training and awareness, it can equally be our greatest liberator and advocator! And when serving the Soul, it becomes a diamond! Brilliant, bright, unshakeable, unstoppable.

Shadow Work. We all have shadow aspects because it's a part of the human experience in a school of polarity. There is both *a shadow within us* as well as *within the collective*. Accepting this is significant and necessary because what we deny or resist will energetically get louder to get our attention. Until its acknowledged, accepted, resolved, and integrated, it will influence us somehow. What triggers us has the capacity to manipulate, coerce or influence us.

Simply put, *the shadow* represents the parts or energies of us that exist in separation and are farther away from the light. They are our wounds, the fractions that need love, acknowledgment, inclusion, comfort, recognition, care, and more.

Interestingly, for various reasons, we have become fearful and averse to acknowledging and facing the parts within us that we deem *ugly, hideous, bad, repulsive, despicable, shameful, unworthy, unlovable, or just plain wrong*. Yet, this is a crucial part of our process to be free.

The irony is that these wounds originated from some experience or perception of pain, separation, loss, rejection, or otherwise. They longingly need our attention, love, and courage to *see* them. By not giving this to them, we perpetuate the original pain of origin. They begin to heal through the process of acknowledging and accepting their existence. **This is the alchemy!** Once admitted, the transformation begins, and the integration commences. We don't get 'rid' of them; we call the pieces back that have been fragmented; we call them home. Like finding a piece of a puzzle, it becomes more complete each time one is added. This is the path of wholeness. This is the path of Freedom.

Higher Mind. As we become more Soul-infused and connected to our hearts, we open up to activating our Divine Mind. An illumined mind brings clear mental thinking. Clear thoughts help us to see what our next step is. We are allowing what is resonating without over-intellectualizing it. Clarity of mind brings clarity of intention, facilitating more of a direction of laser-focused thoughts.

We then have more awareness of our motivation and a deeper understanding of what the *why* is with respect to what it is we want, whom we want to be, and how we want to show up. Most importantly, we are more observant about whether our thoughts support who we want to be and what we want to create. Rather than being run by an outdated narrative that keeps us small, limited, in fear, powerless, helpless, defeated, and definitely not free.

Sometimes, it serves us to understand the *why, when, or how* of something. We can also find ourselves *trying to know*, creating rigidity, constricting the mind, and strengthening the disconnected ego.

Sometimes, the path of *not knowing* opens up the subtle channels of the mind, where we enter into the realm of uncertainty. While this can be very uncomfortable, it is actually a most potent, fertile, and creative space. Clarity births discernment. This helps us with the delicate balance of when we need to surrender to the unknown vs. needing to know.

The Soul is in alignment with the higher mind and facilitates true freedom and independence. This is because when we are Soul-infused, we are self-governing and not dependent on the authority of others. We are free from outside control.

A unified mind is a calm mind. Our head and heart are aligned, and our thoughts reflect the love of our heart. We have a *knowing* that there is nothing to fix. There is just evolution.

From this consciousness, we genuinely have the power to move energy. Our decisions are empowered, and we have the will and ability to direct creative focus.

The mind assists the Soul in creating and birthing our highest potential and the fullest expression of our Divine blueprint into form.

Not only is this our path of freedom, but it is also our path of transcendental evolution!!!

AFFIRMATIONS

I allow myself to pause, breathe and come back to the present moment.

I embrace and love all aspects of myself.

I honor my own unique, true north.

MEDITATION ~ *'I INTEND A SOVEREIGN MIND'*

This meditation can be done lying down or in a comfortable seated position. If seated, place the thumb tips on the index fingertips.

Closing the eyes, take a moment to connect to your breath and body. Inhaling slowly through your nose, exhaling from the nose, releasing any heaviness or tension. Continue this for a few cycles. Visualize that you are in a cocoon of light shaped like a diamond. Now imagine you are the diamond.

Begin to bring awareness to the center of your heart space, which is filled with a beautiful, shimmery color of green. Tune into the quality of love.

Now bring awareness to the center of your mind, filled with a brilliant, shining color of silver. Tune into the quality of wisdom.

(Follow your inner guidance, so if you cannot visualize, set an intention. Example: I intend to align to my heart space and the essence of green at the center of this space. If another color comes up for you, honor it.)

Now imagine the love of your heart, the shade of green flowing up to your mind. The wisdom of your mind, the shade of silver, is now flowing to your heart. Begin to visualize/feel this flow from the heart to mind, mind to heart, becoming a continuous circle of light.

Visualize the colors merging, creating the most brilliant expression of luminescent bright white light. Which is now flowing in a continuous, circular flow of brilliant light, heart to mind, mind to the heart becoming unified/aligned.

(Continue this for 7 mins.)

Visualize yourself again as a diamond, expressing this brilliant white light. Heart and mind unified.

Gently begin to inhale and exhale, bringing slow movement back into your body. Set an intention to go forth and shine your brilliance.

We are One. We are Light. We are Love. We are Free.

(Total 11 minutes. Feel free to shorten or lengthen)

INSIGHTS & JOURNALING OPPORTUNITIES

Freedom 1,2,3

In your own journal or on the pages to follow in this book, take some time to ponder your answers to the following questions.

1. *"Learning to implement a **perspective check** can be invaluable. This is when we pause, asking ourselves how we view, see, and relate to what we are thinking or experiencing."*
   - How do you view yourself? How do you view your relationships?
   - Would it benefit you to see things from a different perspective?
   - How can you see things anew?

2. *"Simply put, **the shadow** represents the parts or energies of us that exist in separation and are farther away from the light. They are our wounds, the fractions that need love, acknowledgment, inclusion, comfort, recognition, care, and more."*
   - How comfortable are you exploring your shadow?
   - What are some shadow aspects or behaviors you can identify?'
   - What do you need to love and embrace your shadow?

3. *"A unified mind is a calm mind. Our head and heart are aligned, and our thoughts reflect the love of our heart. We have a **knowing** that there is nothing to fix. There is just evolution. From this consciousness, we genuinely have the power to move energy. Our decisions are empowered, and we have the will and ability to direct creative focus."*
   - Whom could you be if you were free of any limitations or conditioning?
   - How comfortable are you exploring your shadow?
   - Where do you want to direct your creative focus?

Chapter 8:

Aligning to Our Power of Creation

"Don't look for the solution. Look for the alignment. It will bring the solution."

Abraham Hicks

PARADIGM TERRAIN

Navigating through this paradigm shift can be akin to going to a new country for the first time. We are adjusting to a new time zone, language, customs, and climate. Understanding the terrain we are transitioning into is significant because the game of life is changing. And so are the **principles** and **guidelines**.

Having this understanding will bring awareness as to when we are trying to fit into an old shoe that no longer is the correct size and will bring more excitement, ease, curiosity, and openness to the new way and embrace the change rather than be in fear and resistance.

CONSCIOUS CREATOR

Claiming our sovereignty also activates our evolutionary path of **Conscious Creatorship!** We are constantly creating, and until we have become somewhat conscious of this, we will predominantly create unconsciously from our subconscious and unresolved wounds.

Once we accept that we are an expression of the **Divine Creator** and, therefore, creators in our own right, we need to claim this and assent to the power of authority and responsibility of this **Divine Spark and Power Within.**

Consciously creating happens when we attract and manifest from our hearts. It becomes easier once we learn to identify our egoic narratives and become a Soul-infused personality. Previously we predominantly operated from a place of *shoulds,* duties, obligations, and expectations, or we did it for money, stature, or prestige. Even if it went completely against what we truly wanted to do or be, we would do it anyway. *It was the way of things!*

This new way of being means we now honor our heart's desires and wishes, utilize and express our gifts and talents, and follow our passions. Remember that what we choose will serve the highest good if it's genuinely from Soul alignment. This in and of itself is a significant difference for us and may be difficult for some to understand if entrenched in beliefs that certain customs, lineage, or traditions need to be upheld. While some may choose to continue with some traditions and ways, it can only be in alignment if it's of true inner resonance and the consciousness is aligned to the new paradigm frequency.

Another significant change in how we manifest is that we would set a goal or have an objective to achieve in the past. We would apply our attention and energy until it came into form; the *form or result* was the focus.

Now it's the opposite. We must focus on the *essence* of what we wish to create and manifest. For example, in the past, we would focus on acquiring a specific amount of money (*form/result*), whereas now, we want to ask ourselves, *what is it I'm really seeking*? What does money mean to me? For some, it could be freedom; for others, it could be security or safety. If it's freedom, we want to start giving energy to

freedom if it is what we genuinely want to create. The magnitude
of our desire may still be included in our intention; however, keep in
mind that we may be limiting ourselves by putting a cap on it as the
universe may have more in store for us than we realize. Regardless,
the most important decision is to align with the frequency and
vibration of what we want to experience. In this example, we would
align with freedom.

LAW OF ATTRACTION/LAW OF ASSUMPTION

Conscious Creation blends the law of attraction *(thoughts)* and the
law of assumption *(feelings)*. We want to have focused and positive
thoughts, giving our attention and energy to what we want to create
(*using our example, thinking positive thoughts of freedom and security;
I am free/I am secure*), and we also want to **feel** this.

While thoughts and feelings are intricately connected, the alignment
to the feeling of freedom is critical here. In the past, thinking positive
thoughts, as in the law of attraction, was enough to deliver our
desires. Now there is an additional gateway to honor; it is alignment,
and it is the key to attracting our desires in the new paradigm.
Without it, we will not experience or bring into form our heart's
desires.

When we align to any chosen frequency, we shift the state of our
auric field, the electromagnetic shield around us. Our aura vibrates
what we are projecting and what we are attracting and creating.

To experiment, we can try this; before going into a conversation
or a gathering, we choose what we would like to experience. Let's
say it's kindness. Then we would set an intention to experience
kindness, and we would then *feel* kindness. Hold this vibration for
several seconds to a few minutes before joining the conversation or
connecting to the group. If we are authentically aligned to kindness,

we will receive and be offered kindness.

We want to be mindful that our conscious creating doesn't become conscious controlling. Periodic check-ins with us will help to maintain heart-centered alignment. If we feel body contraction, gripping, or have an expectation or attachment to the outcome (which includes the time it appears and the how), then we have slipped into controlling.

Power of the Word. *The word* is a powerful creation tool. It is considered a deed. The minute it leaves our mouth, *it is creating*. The question is, what are we creating with this highly impactful vibratory expression?

Becoming a conscious creator includes becoming refined with our words *and* how we use them. When speaking from a frequency of honor, reverence, neutrality, and positivity, the words will be uplifting, inspiring, and a blessing.

When we complain, gossip, lie and spew out negativity, we are vomiting out poison. The expression of the word can affect in 3 ways.

1. What we say imprints ourselves.

2. What we send out to the universe comes back to us. (*Cause and effect*)

3. What we say imprints the target person or group.

As we become mindful of this, we can choose our words more wisely and thereby be an instrument of creation rather than destruction.

Co-creating is working as a team with our Soul, spiritual team, and the Universe and has two main components. When we **hear, honor,**

and act on our intuition or inner resonance, we are co-creating.

The other more challenging aspect of co-creating is the alignment to the flow, where we trust and surrender to Divine timing and order, even in the midst of change. For example, we can be in alignment, intending, listening, and acting upon our guidance and moving in a *specific direction* when suddenly, our path detours or shifts direction, like a change in our job or relationship.

Understanding our incarnational blueprint and remembering that our Soul and spiritual team can see from a 360-degree view is essential. If things shift or detour, it may be because it is no longer in our highest good, so keep in mind the intricate choreography, the dynamic movement, and the changeability of life because we are creating as we go. There could be a shift in timelines, our consciousness, or the collective that could create different pathways for us. We are also co-creating with other Souls, therefore, there may be shifts regarding our alignment, and sometimes we may no longer need a specific experience due to our awareness shift.

It can feel like a delicate balance to be consciously creating and co-creating. We do so without abdicating our sovereignty while remaining open and aligned with the flow. Because of this co-creating factor, we may no longer resonate or be able to envision bigger plans and visions. So, learning how to create a surefooted, balanced path includes going moment by moment and experience to experience, honoring and acting upon our inner resonance each step. This means we need to get comfortable with uncertainty and roll with the ebbs and flows of life and our emotions.

The ego may not agree with this at first because to do this requires cooperation and trust in our Soul's guidance and having faith in advance of our results. Remember, when our Soul leads us, we will be guided to thrive rather than be in survival consciousness. It will be a process for us to retrain ourselves to relax and acclimate to this new landscape and its principles. We are creating **elegant equilibrium!**

Even our relationship to time is changing because it is a construct of the previous paradigm (3D). The more we slow down and mindfully allow ourselves to be in the flow, the easier this adjustment will feel. If we try to hurry and rush to get everything done within a specific time frame, we will become restricted and frustrated.

Let's use making a *to-do* list as an example. Previously, we would have set out to check off each item on that list and most often would have felt stressed or pressured about completing it. However, we want to ask ourselves, 'what is my *priority* on this list? We would then set an intention to focus on the priority. If we are in the flow and doing this in a relaxed manner, then amazingly, the other items on the list will be completed. This could be because we naturally had time to accomplish them, they were attended to by someone else, or they no longer needed to be addressed. This is the grace, ease, and joy of aligning with the new paradigm frequencies.

Part of the passage into the new paradigm is learning how to relate to time. Since time is a construct of 3D, we are coming out of the limitations of time. However, because we are still using *time* for appointments, work, or other commitments, we need to learn how to relate differently. For example, say we are expected to be at work at 8 am, and we are behind schedule. Our reactions may include worrying and rushing, which creates frustration, fear, and a focus on lack of time. In contrast, we are learning to slow down, pause, take some deep breaths, and relax the body. This may feel counterproductive at first, as we are acclimatizing to being in the *flow*. In this calmer state, we have the awareness to set an intention and align to the feeling of what it would be like to arrive peacefully at

8 am. Because we've taken the space to pause, align and intend, we are now also creating a trajectory for the rest of the day, which comes from the vibration of calm rather than being frustrated and frazzled.

BEING IN THE FLOW

Because we were previously conditioned to be in survival mode, learning how to be in flow may take some practice.

Imagine that *being in the flow* is like a *moving river.* Visualize standing on the bank of this river, preparing to go into the water. Possibly jumping in, slowly going in, or going in and out a few times before immersing in fully. *(Notice any apprehension or resistance with this/and if water doesn't resonate, visualize an air current.)*

Now in the moving current, imagine we are relaxed on our back and *allowing* ourselves *to be*. The water knows how to go around or over any rocks or obstacles, so we are not fighting, resisting, or trying to go against the stream. We are flowing with it.

TRUSTING THE FLOW; UNDERSTANDING OUR SPIRITUAL TEAM

Co-creating becomes much more conceivable, achievable and meaningful when we develop relationships with *our collaborators*.

Because we are becoming Soul-infused, we don't include our Soul (*Higher Self*) as a part of our spiritual 'team' in this context. We can connect and converse directly with Spirit, Ultimate Creator. And in simple terms, working with the universe is to understand and be in alignment with the laws of the universe and tapping into the potentials in the Quantum Field.

Each of us has a core team with us through each incarnation. Each being, committee, or council has a specific role, function, and purpose and can operate at different levels of consciousness. Some are with us through each incarnation, while others are with us at specific points in our process or levels of consciousness we may be operating from.

High Self is a committee of beings at a very high level of consciousness (like loving wise elders). They are with us through each incarnation, and their purpose is to help us stay aligned to fulfill our incarnational blueprint. They help us create our blueprint by reviewing our past lives with us and providing input on what we intend to learn, heal, accomplish and offer for the upcoming incarnation. *(The term incarnation is referenced rather than lifetime because a Soul can have 'lifetimes lived' within an incarnation.)*

Learning to connect and work with our High Self is incredibly transformative because their wisdom and guidance come from very high levels of consciousness. This means they have a more elevated, comprehensive view and perspective. They also have access to **clear** akashic records. *(Note: High Self differs from Higher Self, our Soul Self.)*

Guardian Angels. Their primary purpose is to protect us and keep us safe. Every incarnated Soul has a High Self committee and Guardian angels.

Additional beings, committees, and councils that are a part of our personal team can vary with us individually. We may acquire certain beings through specific training or initiations. We may also have a certain affinity to particular beings, such as Sophia, Jesus, Shakti, or Buddha. We can also resonate with specific ones while cultivating or needing a certain quality, such as compassion. In this case, we might call in Quan Yin.

There are many categories of beings and guides, all of which may be a part of our team. Some examples include archangels, ascended masters, fairies, spirit animals, intergalactic beings, ancestors (*lineage*), Soul family, and loved ones (*including pets*) that have transitioned, to name just a few.

We can also have masters and specialty guides with us long-term or temporarily, depending on where we are in our process. For example, let's say we are starting a new business or job. We could call in *Masters of Business* or guides specific to the nature of the job we are beginning and ask for their wisdom, support, and guidance.

Communication. The clearer and more specific we are, the better we can be supported. It's also essential that we are requesting beings equal to love and light. Because we are the ones in the body, we want to be mindful that we aren't begging or abdicating, meaning thinking or expecting our spiritual team or Spirit will do things for us or take something away just because we are asking.

We may request support, guidance, and downloads of wisdom, knowledge, and understanding, or we may want to ask to be shown what we need to see or know to heal, transform or bring something to completion.

Although there is the law of grace, there are some things that only those of us incarnated can achieve. Remember that transformation occurs through our experiences, and some experiences may be necessary for our Soul's growth. *(It may also be essential for the evolution of the collective, lineage, or other.)* Therefore, if this is taken away, we would lose our opportunity for growth and, most importantly, the gifts, blessings, and healing that would be birthed upon completion of the particular classroom or experience.

We are learning not to bypass processing our emotions and equally not to avoid our responsibility and honor of being incarnated.

Imagine flying a plane, and our team is in the watch tower. We can't ask them to fly our plane while going through a storm or turbulence. However, we can ask for direction and guidance through it. Sometimes, an event or experience may feel like too much, and we *hand it over* to Spirit or our team. At times, this sacred act of surrender is all we can do, even when we are still attempting to show up on our incarnated end.

For example, if we are going through a period of deep, dark grief and depression. We may not know how or be able to rise out of it. We may *give it to Spirit*, and we maintain our side of things by attending to ourselves as best as possible and engaging back in life when we can.

If we are in a very dark place, we may ask Spirit and our team to lovingly and gently support and guide us through the storm.

An example of how we would still show up in this kind of scenario is to intend to get outside in nature or do some self-care activities each day. If possible, we want to commit something to ourselves, such as going for a 5–20-minute walk daily and then, if needed, give ourselves permission to cry or stay in bed the rest of the day, depending on the depth of the storm. When not able to fulfill that intention or commitment, we want to recommit again without judging or being harsh with ourselves for not being able to hold that commitment. And we keep on building on this until we are eventually out of the storm.

POWER OF NOW

As we awaken to our sovereignty and ignite the birthright of our creatorship, our greatest strength is being fully in the present moment. The new paradigm we are shifting into heralds the time of the **Power of Now!**

Blessing, forgiving, and releasing our past is the freedom gift of self-compassion and peace. Our future is taken care of when we allow ourselves to lovingly be with *what is*, relaxing *into* the moment and not fearing what is next.

The only thing in life that is real is the moment we're in and the way that we feel.

The time has arrived when love prevails, freedom illuminates our path, and infinite kindness and oneness are cultivated!

Sovereign Creators, are we ready to create?

The time is **NOW! HAPPY CREATING!!!**

AFFIRMATIONS

I align to love, peace and freedom.

I trust in Divine Order.

I am FLOW.

MEDITATION ~ *'I INTEND CREATORSHIP'*

Sit in a comfortable, seated position. Straighten the spine. Gently roll the shoulders back and down, opening the heart space. Close the eyes bringing the focus to the Third Eye, the point between the eyebrows.

Place your palms upward and cup them like they are holding water. Hover them a couple of inches above your thighs.

Begin taking a few slow, mindful deep breaths in and out, letting go of anything that is going on in your life—allowing yourself to be fully present to 'You'!

Inhale and slowly bring your cupped palms upward and over your head. As you reach the top of your head, flick the wrists as if you are pouring the water from your cupped palms down your spine.

Exhale and slowly bring the palms back down to hover above your thighs. Continue this in a slow rhythmic cycle.

When inhaling and bringing the palms upward, silently repeat, *I am a Creator*. When exhaling back down, silently repeat, *I am Free*.

(Continue this for 7 mins)

To close, place your left hand on your heart and your right hand over your left. Take a minute and notice how you feel. Feel the creative, shakti energy flowing through you.

Set your intention for the remainder of your day or evening.

We are One. We are Light. We are Love. We are Free.
(Total 11 minutes. Feel free to shorten or lengthen)

INSIGHTS & JOURNALING ~ *Freedom 1,2,3*

In your own journal or on the pages to follow in this book, take some time to ponder your answers to the following questions.

1. *"While thoughts and feelings are intricately connected, the alignment to the feeling of freedom is critical here. In the past, thinking positive thoughts, as in the law of attraction, was enough to deliver our desires. Now there is an additional gateway to honor; it is alignment, and it is the key to attracting our desires in the new paradigm. Without it, we will not experience or bring into form our heart's desires."*
   - What do you want to create and experience?
   - What do you want more of or to expand?
   - How can you support yourself to be in alignment with the frequency you are wanting to experience?

2. *"Power of the Word. The word is a powerful creation tool. It is considered a deed. The minute it leaves our mouth, it is creating. The question is, what are we creating with this highly impactful vibratory expression?"*
   - Are you aware of how you use *the word*?
   - Do you tend to uplift or bring down, bless or curse, speak positively or complain and gossip?
   - Can you feel the difference in your body and energy field when you use different words?

3. *"Co-creating becomes much more conceivable, achievable and meaningful when we develop relationships with our collaborators."*
   - Do you feel connected to your Soul? To Spirit? To your spiritual team?
   - What do you need to cultivate a deeper relationship? How comfortable are you exploring your shadow?
   - Do you have any obstacles or resistance?

Chapter 9:

Coming Home: Welcoming Our Soul

*"As above, so below, as within, so without,
as the universe, so the Soul."*

Hermes Trismegistus

Our journey towards freedom is our path of spiritual maturity, and we experience this individually and collectively. The pillars of this courageous voyage include radical acceptance, understanding, and forgiveness.

SPIRITUAL MATURITY

The Stages of the Ego. Spiritual maturity, our path from unconscious to conscious, includes the development of the ego, noting we aren't seeking the annihilation of the ego and that the ego is not *bad*. We are bringing the ego with us; however, its role is refined and redefined.

Remember that the ego's previous purpose was to lead because we were in *survive consciousness*. As we evolve into the paradigm of *thrive consciousness*, the ego's role now is to serve the heart and Soul.

We are the most unconscious and express our most primitive stage when we have no awareness of the ego. This is when we are fully armored, perceive everything as a threat, and our minds are very closed and rigid. The ego entirely drives our behavior, and protecting the ego *identity* is most important.

As we tune into our inner world, we become more aware of our thoughts, stories, and narratives. We are more conscious of our triggers and are starting to understand that our thoughts are not our Authentic, Soul Selves.

The more we practice self-observation, the more we cultivate the witness/neutral-meditative mind. We are now consistently aware of our triggers and our *stories*. We are now able to respond rather than react.

Once we have learned how to process our emotions and accept our shadow selves, we are now integrating. We are coming into **wholeness**. We no longer need to apply logic to everything or allocate meaning to every experience.

At this point, we become more fully connected to our Soul and Sovereign Self. We will continue to expand from this level of attainment, where we have attained emotional mastery and spiritual maturity because we are continuously evolving and multi-dimensional (*rather than the linear-previous 3D paradigm*).

This is not a process of perfection where we completely get it. The platform we arrive at becomes the new foundation from which we now begin to uplevel and develop to the next stage of consciousness or rung on the spiral.

This blooming will unfold in our Soul Divine timing for each of us. The most beautiful gift we can offer ourselves and others during this unfolding is to be gentle, patient, and kind. And humor is **always** valuable.

BREAKING OUT OF THE LOOP OF VICTIMIZATION

Claiming Our Sovereignty. Our emergence to liberation coincides with dismantling the cycles of suffering so deeply programmed within us and part of the collective matrix.

Healing the Paradox. To our Soul, there is no *victim*. Therefore, claiming our sovereignty requires learning how to release blame. **Perhaps one of the most heroic acts we will ever do in our evolutionary journey is to transcend the victim archetype.**

Because we have been conditioned and trained to be in victim consciousness, it has become an imprinted stain on our DNA and psyche. *Victimhood* is the sticky glue that keeps the programming of bondage in place in the matrix.

The perplexity of this stage of our maturation is that there are still unthinkable injustices and atrocities being carried out on our planet. Additionally, we may have personal memories, traumas, abuses, outrages, and cruelties that we are still reeling and healing from. The solution and the healing balm to this fractured construct and pervasive darkness is to transcend this and rise to embrace and claim our **Power of Choice!**

We have the **inner authority** to choose *love* over *fear*, *understanding* over *hate, kindness* over *cruelty*, and *freedom* over *subjugation*. Our sovereignty is activated when we **consciously decide to choose**, even if we aren't ready or want to choose love or understanding, or we don't yet believe we can ever be free! When we **intentionally choose**, whatever that is, we are **self-governing**. We are not being managed by anything outside our internal command. We are connecting to the true source of our power and freedom within.

We are not allowing helplessness and hopelessness to defeat or squash our light and dignity.

It matters. **And it makes a difference.**

As energy starts to move, we begin to shift. Massive transformation results from the small steps and consistently choosing, one decision at a time. Often, we will look back and be unable to recall precisely when the change's origin happened. We will have an awareness of how evolved and transformed we have become.

If we **choose to open and align with becoming a Soul-infused personality,** a *both/and* perspective will become foundational. For example, we may still be hurting or angry from injustice, **and** we are open to forgiving that person/group/experience. (*This doesn't mean that we know how or when that will happen at this time, but we are open to it.*)

There is concurrent processing of emotions such as pain, grief, or anger and an openness and intention to transcend the suffering, trauma, drama, or story. By choosing to seek freedom, peace, or forgiveness, we can transcend the *blame game*. If we continue to fuel the negative emotion, we prolong the classroom and delay our growth.

The paradox is that we cannot claim our sovereignty if we are in a state of victimhood or blame. We are healing victim consciousness when we no longer operate from this deep-seated programming and conditioning.

An additional challenge lies in the possibility that there won't be acknowledgment or release from the person or group that has been the transgressor. We often stay in anger, grief, and frustration because we feel that until we have justice or compensation, we cannot move through and beyond the act of what happened or resolve the residing pain. There may be a part of us in righteousness, and we may not want to heal until there has been rectitude and restoration of honor.

The other side of this coin is being able to release guilt or shame for ourselves when we have been the transgressor. True freedom also means gifting ourselves with the compassion and space needed to learn and evolve the experience. For this to occur, self-forgiveness is required.

Attaining the level of consciousness where we can accept, understand and forgive requires the grace of being a Soul-infused personality. Through the alignment and surrender to the guidance of our Higher Self, we can now perceive what's possible and understand that all is achievable from the presence of love. Without bypassing the reality of what is or has been, nor the wounding of our shadow.

From this clarity, we can remember and comprehend that all life is sacred, which creates the ability to pierce beyond the veils and darkness to see the fabric of Divine intelligence that flows through all life, beings, and experiences.

An example of how we may experience this is imagining walking along the same pathway every day. Maybe it's a long driveway, and we are going to the mailbox at the end, or perhaps it's a path we take to work or the store. Along or beside this pathway is a muddy, dirty pit filled with jagged and ugly rocks.

We never feel good looking upon or strolling past this eyesore. It appears and feels as if it is lifeless, barren, dark, and empty until one day, something shifts, and we suddenly see a sparkle of light in the pit. It's so quick and subtle that we may even think we have imagined it. Yet we have a *knowing* we saw it. So, we begin to pierce more profoundly into the pit and realize that diamonds are embedded in the rough rocks. The more we see them, the brighter they become, and we are stunned by the fact that we've never seen them before.

Eventually, we drum up the courage to go into the pit and begin to extract these brilliant diamonds. Until, to our amazement, one day, the pit is transformed into a bright ocean of light and luminosity.

This analogy is synonymous with the alchemy of our transformative process and the power of our union with our Soul and Spirit. The unseen becomes seen when we choose to be open, curious, and willing. The impossible becomes possible. We have become new. The world as we know it has become new. Hope arises for our future generations. A new world begins to be created. Our species is leaping into a new evolution. A new day is dawning!

Such is the power of an open, willing heart and a Soul-infused personality.

Such is the power of radical acceptance, understanding, and forgiveness!

Radical Acceptance. It is called radical because of our programming of separatism and suffering. Acceptance will most often feel like we are going against our self-preservation. We may also associate it with a belief or perception that we are *weak* to do so or that we are *condoning* or *consenting* to the injustice, act, or transgression, which is **not the case!**

When we let go of resistance and denial of *what is,* and we release resentment, bitterness, conflict, and the need to be correct, we allow movement to ensue. As energy begins to flow, solutions come through. We start to see angles and are open to previously unavailable perspectives.

Radical acceptance fosters radical kindness when we see that everything has value. From this place, we begin to ask, *what would kindness do in this situation?*

Understanding. This is potentially one of the most life-changing Soul qualities we can seek and cultivate because a more profound internal shift begins once we are open to seeing things from different perspectives. Once we perceive and comprehend different *levels, layers, shades, and hues*, other Soul qualities such as love, compassion and forgiveness occur naturally.

Forgiveness. This is truly a gift of **self-compassion** because this act brings us *home and into connectivity,* into our hearts, and in alignment with our Soul Self.

Arriving here, ready, willing, and able to make a **conscious choice** to release feelings of resentment, bitterness, vengeance, and hatred towards another person, group, culture, sub-culture, and self, **we are free from the bondage of separation and victim consciousness.**

When we hold back forgiveness, including to self, we cultivate a distrust of the potential of love and connectivity—creating more separation and suffering.

To **authentically forgive** is to have an actual **shift in energy at the subconscious level**. A transmutation or transformation occurs, allowing us to be neutral about the person, group, or situation.

We can't fool energy! Understanding, intellectualizing, burying, or desiring it isn't enough to be in authentic forgiveness. The energy, right down to the subconscious, needs to be addressed, transformed, and transmuted.

Once this transpires, we achieve spiritual maturity, where the cycle of suffering breaks. From here, we can genuinely be open-hearted, kind, compassionate, and into the consciousness of togetherness.

The walls dissolve, and we feel safe, secure, grounded, and peaceful. Arriving here brings us to our most authentic, profound Presence!

We are in the full claiming and responsibility of our **Creatorship! Our Sovereign Self!**

From here, we are liberated! We are Free! From here, we can Create a New Earth! Where all beings are Free! Where Peace and Love Reign!

Evolution from victim to freedom: *Victim… Acceptance… Understanding… Forgiveness… Liberation… Freedom*

THE SELFLESS JOURNEY: THE PATH INWARD

Forgiveness is much easier when we accept our *weaknesses and shadows* as part of the learning process. This is why exploring our inner landscape is vital. The more we know *who we are*, the more we can show up for ourselves, others, and our planet. Our inbound journey awakens us to our true and **Authentic Self!**

One common block to this pursuit is the fear that what we discover may be too much, too overwhelming, and painful.

We may feel we don't deserve to take the time and space for this form of self-care. Moreover, we have many beliefs and conditioning that it's selfish to do so!

The irony is that this sacred passage facilitates our remembering of *home* and returning to our true essence of Love! An authentic, introspective voyage connects us to our Higher Self; in this alignment, we naturally become more caring and considerate for all life! All beings! We ground into the consciousness of togetherness! Therefore, it isn't just motivation for one's gain. Even though, at first, it may feel like it's a selfish path, feeling that others will judge us as selfish indicates the presence of codependency.

Cultivating Stillness. Our inward journey of discovery brings us into the realm of the creative, fertile womb of infinite creativity, where inspiration and imagination are ignited, and all becomes possible.

130

This intimate odyssey cultivates stillness, facilitating equanimity amongst many other gifts, including the power of presence or magnetism and the subtle cognizance of what is unseen, including a deeper connection to all life and beings and a brilliant, energetic vibrancy!

The limitations imposed by our five senses and the illusionary curtain of the matrix begin to fall away. We begin to be able to perceive the connections rather than the separation.

We begin to understand the universal flow, the sacred gift of life, and newfound gratitude emerges. We can perceive our world through a reverent and clear lens of unity, freedom, harmony, and congruence.

When we align to the universe and our Soul, we flow easily into the natural rhythm of the ebb and flow of life and our transformational process. It's our journey to Freedom.

Like flowing rivers navigating their way back to the oceans, so too are we finding our way back home, to our Sovereignty!

The time of Freedom is upon us!

What will you choose, Magnificent Creator?

What will you Create?

AFFIRMATIONS

I am one with all.

I forgive! I am free!

I am home in my Soul.

MEDITATION ~ '*I INTEND ONENESS*'

This meditation can be done lying down or in a comfortable seated position. If seated, place the thumb tips on the index fingertips. Close the eyes and connect to the breath, inhaling and exhaling slowly for a few cycles. (Eye gaze can be on the Third Eye space, between the eyebrows, or relaxed.)

Bring your awareness to your heart space, inhaling now from the heart, exhaling from the heart. Continue this heart breath for a few cycles.

Begin to call forth your Soul. Or expand more into your Soul. Ask to feel its presence, love, strength, and peace. Sit quietly for a moment in the presence of your Divine Soul Self. (It's okay if you don't feel anything, calling forth and intending is enough)

Intend Beingness, Oneness, Wholeness! Ask this process to be done gently and lovingly.

Focus on the steady rhythm of your breath and the presence of your Soul. Begin to call back any fragments of your Soul and personality self, including inner child aspects ready to be healed and integrated. Including all that is seen and unseen, known and unknown, conscious and unconscious. From all lives, realities, layers, levels, and dimensions. From all creational origin points of trauma, conflict, separation, pain, suffering, and discord.

Ask that all your energies scattered in the Universe that you have given away through your thoughts and attention is brought back to you; any energies you have knowingly or unknowingly been drained from you are brought back to you. Ask that all energies that can now come back to you, right here, right now, in this time and space, be brought back to you as usable energy. That you are brought back into wholeness, peace, and harmony. Ask that you remember who you are. Sit/Be in Silence (7 mins or as long as you feel a resonance to do so)

To close, Place one hand on your heart and one on your lower belly.

Repeat 'I AM' 3x. Set your intention!

We are One. We are Light. We are Love. We are Free.
(Total 11 minutes. Feel free to shorten or lengthen)

132

INSIGHTS & JOURNALING ~ *Freedom 1,2,3*

In your own journal or on the pages to follow in this book, take some time to ponder your answers to the following questions.

1. *"An additional challenge lies in the possibility that there won't be acknowledgment or release from the person or group that has been the transgressor. We often stay in anger, grief, and frustration because we feel that until we have justice or compensation, we cannot move through and beyond the act of what happened or resolve the residing pain."*

    - Are you harboring resentment or bitterness towards anyone or anything?
    - Do you feel open to forgiveness? Is there anything holding you back?
    - What do you need to begin the process of forgiveness? What quality could you focus on to strengthen your process?

2. *"The other side of this coin is being able to release guilt or shame for ourselves when we have been the transgressor. True freedom also means gifting ourselves with the compassion and space needed to learn and evolve the experience. For this to occur, self-forgiveness is required."*

    - Is there anything needing forgiveness within you and your relationship with yourself?
    - Are there blocks, obstacles, or resistance preventing you from forgiving yourself?
    - What qualities could you focus on to begin your process of self-forgiveness?

3. *"When we align to the universe and our Soul, we flow easily into the natural rhythm of the ebb and flow of life and our transformational process. It's our journey to Freedom."*

    - Where are you in alignment?
    - Where do you want/need more alignment?
    - Do you relate to yourself as a *sovereign being*?

JOURNAL & REFLECTION

*Allow The Whispers Of
Your Soul & Spirit
To Flow*

RESOURCES

Ego Power - Heart Power Examples
Supportive Self Care Tools/Techniques
Soul Qualities Chart
Affirmations

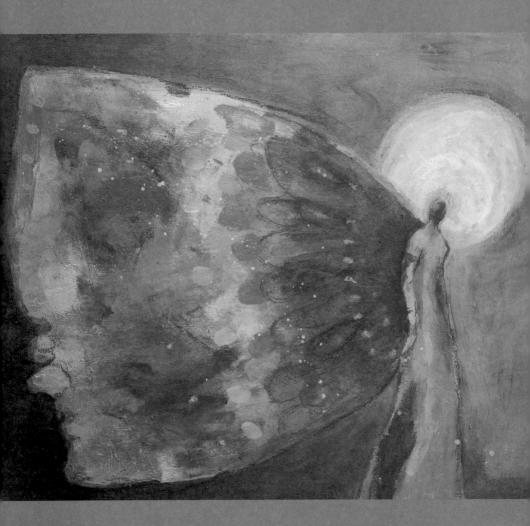

Ego Power - Heart Power

Ego Power	Heart Power
Finite	Infinite
Disconnected	Connected
Limited	Unlimited
Fosters Fear	Fosters Love
Imbalanced 3rd Chakra	Opened Heart Chakra
Manipulation	Empowered
Greed/Lack	Abundance/Plenty
Coercion	Freedom
Listen to Outer Influences	Listen to Inner Resonance
Judgment	Acceptance
Separatism	Unity
Exclusion	Inclusion
Inequality	Equality
Injustice	Justice
Abuse	Respect
Emphasis on Status/Prestige	Emphasis Honoring Gifts/Talents
I Should	I Know
Competition	Collaboration
Misaligned	Aligned
Self Serving	We Serving
Force	Flow
Cultivates War	Cultivates Peace
Hate	Compassion
Conflict	Harmony
Chasing	Attracting
Blame	Responsibility
Materialism	Fulfillment Within
Complaining	Gratitude
Past/Future Oriented	Present Moment
Hostility	Friendliness

Supportive Self Care Tools/Techniques

Common indications that self-nurturing is needed or to be increased is when we are feeling frazzled, overwhelmed, short-fused, feeling oversensitive, disconnected, and pushing through to name just a few.

The benefits are many. The calmer and more relaxed we are, the clearer we are to connect to our inner guidance. Therefore, we can be more of a conscious creator and make choices based on what will support our highest good and fulfillment.

Learning to tune into what we need and honoring that need is one of the most loving things we can do for ourselves. This includes asking our body, personality, mind, and Soul what is needed. The body may need rest. The Soul may need peace. The mind may need to repeat positive affirmations. The personality may need to laugh.

Creating a daily practice of connecting inward facilitates being more aware, grounded, and connected to our inner guidance and body. This could range from daily meditation or journaling or quietly sitting in silence for 5 minutes. The key is to cultivate a regime that feels doable, and that we can create consistency with. So, 5 minutes daily may be more effective than trying to do an hour which ends up feeling too overwhelming and grueling and we end up not sticking with it.

It is also very advantageous to create a few non-negotiables for ourselves. This can help us stay true and committed to ourselves and our highest well-being. For example, if we are a vegetarian, a non-negotiable would be to not eat meat. Because that is what resonates from deep within. Or it could be we won't skip breakfast because it wreaks havoc on our emotional and energetic stability.

Under certain circumstances, we may also want to add smaller check-ins throughout the day, which could be as simple as setting a reminder every couple of hours to tune into our heart space and take a couple of deep, mindful breaths in and out.

The purpose of self-nurturing practices is they are life-giving. Bringing renewal, rejuvenation, and connection to our Soul, heart, and life. Restoring lightness, passion, and purpose. They facilitate increasing and maintaining higher frequencies. They bring joy, peace, and comfort. We are brought back home, inward to ourselves. We are increasing or maintaining our Chi, our Divine Nectar.

The key is that we are customizing it to our unique selves.

Examples of Supportive Self Nurturing Techniques

Spend time in nature

Breath work

Meditation

Mindful Walking

Journaling

Rest

Exercise/Activity-moving the body

Healthy nutrition

Sufficient intake of water

Sunlight

Baths

Gardening

Music

Dancing

Sitting quietly with self

Being creative

Writing or reading poetry

Watching favorite movies

Yoga/Chi gong/Tai Chi

Laughter

Trying something new

Reading

Write 50 superpowers (I am friendly, kind, passionate....)

Setting intentions

Being loving to the body

Complimenting self

Positive self talk

Connecting with crystals

Using essential oils

Support with Bach flowers

Eating favourite meal

Cooking

Relaxation

Connecting with an old friend

Spa night

Sacred ceremony

Being in silence

Watch a thunderstorm

Foot massage before bed

Keep space clean and organized

Spend time with or around animals

Showers (asking for any negative or heavy energies to be cleansed and released)

Eat regular meals

Mindful of energetic intakes (news, violence, etc.)

Practice positive emotions

Repeat affirmations

Bare feet in the grass

Create a cozy space

Connect to your Soul

Recorrect alignment (feel love, peace, etc.)

Oracle cards

Bless food and water

Affirmations

I have the power to choose.

Sovereignty (freedom) is my Divine birthright.

I am free to rise and thrive.

I am love.

I bless and release that which no longer serves me.

I allow myself to feel to heal.

I am courageous and I choose to grow from all experiences.

I am a creator and can rewrite my stories.

I trust my inner resonance.

I am the Power and Presence of the Divine.

My path is illuminated before me.

I am worthy! I am enough!

I call forth my Soul.

I surrender to the grace and guidance of my Soul.

I choose Love.

I intend to unify my mind with the Divine mind.

I am beautiful, unique, and blessed.

I am a Divine diamond.

I allow myself to pause, breathe &come back to the present moment.

I embrace and love all aspects of myself.

I honor my own unique, true north.

Soul Qualities

Abundance
Acceptance
Awareness
Beauty
Benevolence
Caring
Cheerfulness
Clarity
Cleanliness
Comfort
Compassion
Composure
Concern
Confidence
Consideration
Constructiveness
Control
Courage
Courtesy
Creativity
Desire
Determination
Direction
Endurance
Enthusiasm
Faith
Forgiveness
Freedom
Friendliness
Generosity
Gentleness
Giving freedom

Grace
Gratitude
Happiness
Harmony
Health
Helpfulness
Honesty
Hope
Hospitality
Humility
Innocence
Intelligence
Involvement
Joy
Justice
Kindness
Listening
Laughter
Life
Love
Love of God
Love of life
Love of men
Love of self
Love of women
Loyalty
Mercy
Obedience
Optimism
Order
Passiveness
Patience

Peace
Perseverance
Prosperity
Punctuality
Purpose
Relaxation
Responsibility
Restraint
Self-esteem
Reverence
Self-control
Self-forgiveness
Selflessness
Self-preservation
Sincerity
Sobriety
Strength
Success
Supportiveness
Sympathy
Tact
Thoughtfulness
Tolerance
Trust
Truthfulness
Understanding
Unity
Vitality
Wholeness
Wisdom
Worthiness

From Suffering to Joy!
The light within me
honors the light within you.
It is truly an immense
joy to journey alongside
you on this courageous
voyage! In deep gratitude
+ love. Cathrine

As we journey through our
lives and experience deep
contrasts in this school of
polarity, I am grateful
for the kind and gentle
souls who share their
love and light with me,
both energetically and
physically. Our souls
are connected now too ♡
Life is good. xo melissa

We see this book as much more than its physical presence!

We see it as an invitation!

✦ Read the book, experience the meditations, use the affirmations
✦ Open your heart as you work through the insights & journaling
✦ Seek out opportunities to intentionally integrate your insights
   and learnings into your daily living

We created the **Freedom & Flow Spiritual Resource Centre** to
inspire, guide, and support the transformation of kind-hearted,
growth-oriented, like-minded Souls. Join us as you journey within,
step into your highest purpose, and awaken your potential.

CathrineMarshall.com/FreedomAndFlow

Melissa-Lyons.com/FreedomAndFlow

Hi! I am Cathrine Marshall, and I have had the profound honor and privilege of serving and facilitating the healing of thousands of Souls for over 33 years. As I continue my own lifelong transformation, I am grateful to cross paths with you and your own beautiful and courageous journey.

I can recall, even as a young child being very sensitive to the suffering of others, and all beings. A pivotal and transformational marker transpired for me when I was 8. I experienced an 'earthquake' in my life when my parents, in alignment with their own souls' journey, decided to divorce. This would begin the foundation of my path and set the stage for me to embark on the archetypal path of the Heroine's Journey.

When I was 14, I experienced several deaths and losses, which occurred at the same time my abstract thinking was activating. These events became a catalyst of awakening and began a deep, life-long quest of yearning to understand the deeper meaning of life and death, particularly why we suffer and experience such depths of pain.

An inner trajectory brought about more significant and painful experiences (law of attraction), thereby providing many circumstances that birthed deeper understanding, compassion, and kindness. These experiences brought challenges, losses, and tribulations on every single level of my life, including significant personal trauma, loss and near-death experience.

Interestingly, after each experience, I was prompted to explore ways to facilitate my healing and gain deeper insight and understanding of what had transpired. As a result, I have an in-depth education and training in Psychology, Spirituality, Yoga, Meditation, Homeopathy, Yogic Numerology, SRT, and many other profound Soul-healing arts.

My path has led me to who I am today. I serve as a metaphysical energetic healer, guide, and author. I hold space of gentleness and support to facilitate awakening, ease weariness, and re-inspire and flame the light within others as they birth a new love of self and life.

I have created an online educational and spiritual center designed to facilitate empowering personal and global transformation. It includes transformative courses such as Numerology and healing workshops such as Bach Flower Healing Therapy, supportive and rejuvenating meditations, along with podcasts of shared wisdom.

Through one-on-one sessions, workshops, courses, and books, my passionate work alleviates suffering and inequality, conduiting the opening of the heart, and sparking the flame of love, compassion, freedom, and peace within. This supports and nurtures one's process and alchemy in a gentle yet powerful way. My clients awaken, hear, honor, and claim their Soul Power, Divinity, and Sovereignty.

We are One. We are Light. We are Love. We are Sovereign.

Connect: cathrinemarshall.com / hello@cathrinemarshall.com

Hi! I am Melissa Lyons, and I am honored to share this precious moment with you.

What brought you here? What life events happened for you to lead you to this time and place?

For me, my now is this... I am a sensitive and loving Soul. I am a mother, a wife, a daughter, a sister, a friend, and a lover of all sorts of adventures. I am an international best-selling author and an Intuitive Life Coach specializing in self-discovery. I love helping people find the answers to life's most challenging questions, including 'Why is this happening to me?', 'How can I recover?' and 'How can I create more meaning in my life?'.

I have been described as raw and relatable, and I understand why. Throughout my life, I have experienced pain, loss, emotional distress, deep disappointments, and extended periods of self-loathing. At one point in the midst of my darkness, I made the choice to find my light. I hit bottom and finally said to myself, Enough! That's enough!

And here I am. I have learned what it means to surrender. I have discovered how to redirect my thoughts and experiences in almost any given moment, and I am able to realign with my Soul's plan and find my center and connect to freedom, peace, love, and joy.

Throughout the decades of my entrepreneurial and corporate business experience, I was always searching for something.

Something more...something different. Something I couldn't put into words. This yearning inspired me to question my life purpose and fueled my search for more meaning and fulfillment.

It warms my heart to know that my books, programs, retreats, and coaching have helped tens of thousands heal and find peace in their hearts and minds. If you are searching for more or less of anything in your life, I invite you to explore some of my offerings.

My gifts and passions facilitate transformation through implementation, integration, and bringing everything back to the precious present. Knowing (information) is the first step. Living and integrating your knowledge is the momentum needed to create the life you are meant to live.

> *"The only thing in life that is real is the moment you're in and the way that you feel."*

It was during an intense journaling session that I wrote my first book. It was an unexpected miracle that changed the trajectory of my life and the lives of many. Here are my first two books. They offer instrumental healing and comfort for people of all ages.

- *I Will Always Love You*, *A Journey From Grief and Loss to Hope and Love* – Hardcover & Journal Formats
- *Until We Meet Again*, *From Grief to Hope After Losing a Pet*

Connect: melissa-lyons.com / melissa@melissa-lyons.com

Kerri McCabe is a full time intuitive artist.

From her studio in the Pacific Northwest she works intently, using her connection to her inner guidance to build abstract figurative work that mainly centers on mankind's ever present need for connection to a world larger and grander than what we experience with our physical five senses. Trusting in that spiritual guidance each of her paintings move through layers of seemingly random mark making until a cohesive whole is revealed. Usually, at that point a title is given, and only then does the artist know what the painting is about. It is always a joy to know that trust has been rewarded with something unexpected but also illuminating.

Kerri has sold hundreds of paintings world wide and is held in private and public collections. Her work has also been distributed through retail purveyors such as Crate and Barrel. But her main passion is connecting with collectors directly. Connection, after all, is what her work is all about.

Connect: ArtistKerriMcCabe.com

Freedom Rising From Within

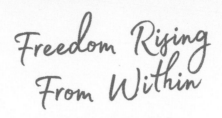

Bonus Access!

We have some special gifts to share!
All meditations can be listened to as guided
meditations and all of the journaling & reflection
exercises are available as digital downloads.

You can access them for free through either of our websites.

CathrineMarshall.com/FreedomRisingGifts

Melissa-Lyons.com/FreedomRisingGifts

And There Is More!

We Lovingly Invite You To Explore Our
Freedom & Flow Spiritual Resource Centre

Freedom & Flow
Spiritual Resource Centre

An Online Community Welcoming
Kind-Hearted, Growth-Oriented,
Like-Minded Souls

A Soul-Inspired program created to inspire, guide,
and support your journey within so that you may:

Remember Who You Are
Awaken To Your Potential
Understand Your Divine Blueprint
Fulfill Your Path of Highest Purpose

More Details...

CathrineMarshall.com/FreedomAndFlow

Melissa-Lyons.com/FreedomAndFlow

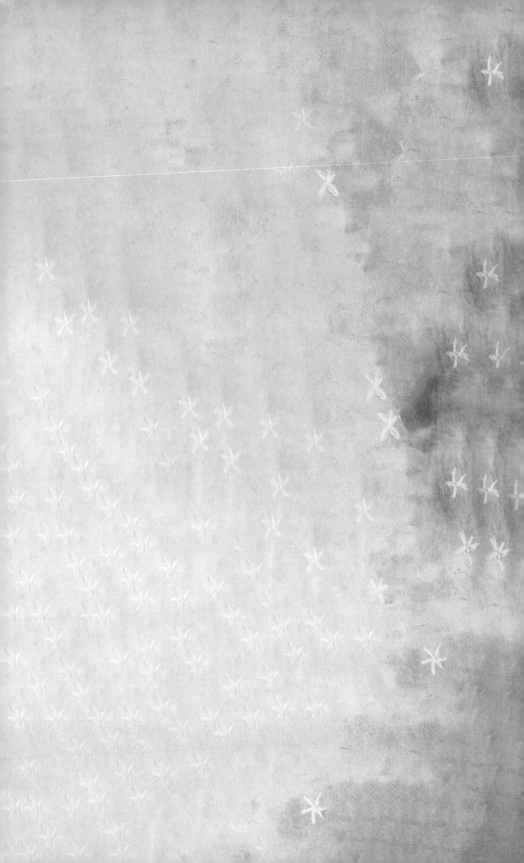